COLLAGE

JOURNEYS

The play house

DEAN DAWNE
1. ~~Tom~~ and ~~Betty~~

have a play house.

2. This is the play house.

3. This is the little play house.

DEAN
4. Find ~~Betty~~.

DAWNE
5. Find ~~Tom~~.

6. Find the play house.

12.—The Fun we used to Have.

āim, purpose.
är·chi·tĕc·tūre, art of building.
e·mē̇rġ·ing, coming out.
bŭr·rō̇wed, dug into.
do·mĕs'tie, home-like.

NEW YORK
Long Isla
SCALE OF MILE
1 2 3 4

the joy of the

PLAY HOUSE

COLLAGE
JOURNEYS

A PRACTICAL GUIDE TO
CREATING PERSONAL ARTWORK

JANE DAVIES

WATSON-GUPTILL PUBLICATIONS / NEW YORK

All rights reserved.
Published in the United States by Watson-Guptill Publications, an imprint of the Crown Publishing Group,
a division of Random House, Inc., New York.
www.crownpublishing.com
www.watsonguptill.com

ISBN-10: 0 8230 9951 2
ISBN-13: 978 0 8230 9951 1

Library of Congress Control Number: 2008923515

Watson-Guptill Publications books are available at special discounts when purchased in bulk for premiums and sales promotions, as well as for fundraising or educational use. Special editions or book excerpts can be created.

Executive editor: Joy Aquilino
Editor: Patricia Fogarty
Designer: Chin-Yee Lai and Wendy Lai
Production director: Alyn Evans

Photography by John Polak and George Bouret
Opposite the title page: "The Joy of the Play House," by Dawne Polis

Manufactured in China

First printing, 2008

3 4 5 6 7 8 9 / 15 14 13 12 11 10

CONTENTS

Collage by Jane Davies

Collage by Autumn Hathaway

INTRODUCTION

———————————

Collage is a vibrant and exciting medium that is particularly well suited to the process of personal expression. It requires no special artistic "skill," just a willingness to jump in and explore the possibilities. The immediacy of collage gets at the heart of the creative process, putting images and textures together with an open mind and a sense of adventure. It is not about making pretty pictures in a technically proficient way. It is about trusting your intuitive visual and conceptual associations, and using collage as a tool for self-expression.

I recently heard author Richard Russo say that he writes books for the same reason that he reads them: to find out what happens. To me, collage is like that. You don't know where you will end up when you start, and the journey is a process of discovery. That is why I call collage a *journey*. It is not the end product, or the destination, that is of primary importance. Rather, it is the process, rich with the unexpected.

First, we'll look at the vast array of materials, from everyday ephemera to your own handmade collage papers. We'll also cover the basics of supports and adhesives. Throughout the remaining chapters we'll explore various approaches to the collage process, including projects and exercises that can help you along your collage journey.

If you are new to collage or have been away from art-making for a long period of time, I would suggest paying particular attention to chapter 2, which gives you a set of ongoing practices that can help you generate ideas and feed your creative spirit. If you are an art journaler, chapter 7 presents collage journaling projects, including making your own journals by hand. No matter what your starting point, you are sure to find inspiration and ideas from the many wonderful collage artists represented in this book.

GATHERING MATERIALS

Exercise your intuitive resonance with visual and tactile stimuli. Your materials can stimulate associations of imagery, color, texture, and text.

Gathering materials for collage can be as much fun and as stimulating as the process of making collage. Students of mine have said that making collage from a wide variety of papers and ephemera changes the way they look at everything. Suddenly you can see the potential for collage in every piece of gluable substance that meets your eye. Hunting and gathering is an ongoing artistic survival skill. Part of keeping your creative self alive and nurtured is exercising your intuitive resonance with visual and tactile stimuli. Simply choosing to save *this* piece of ephemera and not *that* one is a creative act.

The materials you gather and create can be a rich source of inspiration, stimulating ideas and associations of imagery, color, texture, and text that you may otherwise not have thought of. Sometimes one collage material will suggest a whole series of pieces, or send you out on a hunt for related imagery. The materials you choose set the tone of the collage you create, even if, in the process, the original materials become completely obscured.

Many of the materials we will discuss are not archival, or acid-free. This means that they will eventually show their age by fading, yellowing, or becoming brittle. However, if you use archival paper as your support, or apply a coat of gesso or matte medium to another kind of support (such as fabric or wood), your piece should last for decades without visible deterioration. Another way to improve the longevity of your collages is to use archival adhesives (see the section on adhesives, page 17) and/or acrylic mediums for adhering materials to your support.

Found materials
Old photographs, books, magazine pages, and maps are among the many found materials used in collage.

SUPPORTS

**Support material affects the character
of a finished collage.**

A support is the substrate onto which your collage is built. The material you choose for a support affects the character of your finished collage to varying degrees. If you cover the entire surface of your support with collage materials, as I usually do, then the aesthetic quality of the support's surface may not be relevant (just make sure that it will bond with the adhesive you are using). However, its thickness and weight are important to the look of the finished piece.

I usually use a medium-weight, smooth-surfaced watercolor or printmaking paper for my support. It is heavy enough for most collage and paint applications, and is inexpensive and easily accessible. This kind of paper will suffice for most of the projects in this book. If you want a heavier support, you can use illustration board, mat board, or even ordinary cardboard, which, however, is not archival, or acid-free, and will yellow and disintegrate with time. Wood gives a nice weight and dimension to a collage when used as a support (see "House Dream," on page 88). First, sand the wood and seal it with gesso, acrylic medium, or paint. Stretched canvas and canvas board are also good choices; see "My Sister and I Were Close Like That," "House Floating," and one of my collage studies (all on page 86), as well as the

examples of acrylic glaze over stretched canvas and canvas board (page 76).

Fabric makes an interesting support because of its texture and drape (see "Riding to . . ."). Sometimes I use plain muslin stiffened with matte medium. To prepare fabric for use as a support, iron it onto a sheet of freezer paper (use a piece of scrap fabric or paper to protect your iron and ironing board). This stiffens the fabric enough to paint and collage on it. Once your acrylic paint and collage elements have dried, peel away the freezer paper. Sharon McCartney's "Marking Home" (page 12) is a lovely example of a collage done on linen. For a more heavily textured fabric support, try taking discarded paintings (your own or some flea-market finds) and cutting the canvas off the stretcher, as I did in "Untitled (canvas houses)" (page 12). You can either use the painted image as a starting point for your collage, or gesso over it and start with a blank, but textured, support.

Chapter 7 looks at books as supports for collage.

I have recently been inspired by Carol Owen (*Crafting Personal Shrines: Using Photos, Mementos & Treasures to Create Artful Displays*, Lark Books, 2004) to use foam board wrapped in paper as a support for collage; see, for example, "Simplicity" (page 13). I use it for many of my artist trading cards (ATCs), including "Group of ATCs" (page 23) and "Gone Fishing" (page 24), and for my Collage-a-Day practice (see page 43 and my small foam-core collages shown as illustrations for the project).

Ericka Schmidt: From her "Unfolding" series, 40˝ x 26˝
Because Erika leaves a lot of her support surface exposed as part of the overall composition, her choice of support is as important as her choice of collage materials.

Jane Davies: Riding to . . . , 11˝ x 8 ½˝
I printed out a digitally altered image from a Greek vase painting onto printable cotton fabric and used that as my support. After applying a coat of matte medium to the fabric support, I layered more printed fabric imagery, printed papers, and paint to complete my image.

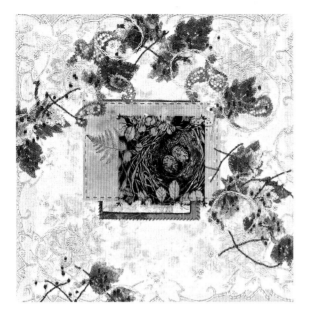

This kind of everyday ephemera has a real connection to our lives. A ticket stub says that you went to a movie or traveled on a train or plane; a receipt is a record of something you bought; a grocery list gives a glimpse of what you keep in your pantry or how you cook and eat. These little pieces of paper can remind us of our ordinary, everyday activities, or recall places we've traveled or people we've seen or heard from.

FOUND MATERIALS:
EVERYDAY EPHEMERA

Pieces of everyday ephemera have real connections to your life.

You can start saving ephemera from your daily life: receipts, movie tickets, cocktail napkins, matchbooks, postcards, gift wrap, junk mail, non-junk mail, newspaper clippings, candy or food wrappers, telephone messages, doodles, etc. Anything that comes into your life that can be glued to a surface is fair game. Before throwing such ephemera into the recycling bin, take a quick look to see if there are any interesting tidbits that could be used in collage. Graphic type, images, textures, colors or surfaces can often be found in the most mundane litter of our lives.

Jane Davies: Untitled (canvas houses), 14″ x 10″
I used a previously stretched and painted canvas as the support for this highly textured collage.

Jane Davies: Simplicity, 8 1/2″ x 5 1/2″
This piece was created on a foam-core support. To learn how to make a recess in a foam-core support, see "Making a Foam-Core Frame for an ATC" (page 25).

Project:
Daily-Life Collage

**Play with materials to stimulate
your creativity.**

This exercise is designed to allow you to play with materials and to stimulate your creativity. Doing it in a group is a lot of fun and allows members of the group to share materials from each other's stashes. Whether you do it on your own or with others, gather a collection of materials from your daily life as described on page 12. Then follow three basic steps.

1. Lay down a background (see chapter 4) or use one of your daily-life materials as the background. Or start with a page in your journal.

2. Arrange and rearrange your chosen ephemera on the background until you have a pleasing composition. Glue it to the support. You could stop right there or take the process further by adding some color with acrylic paint or water-soluble crayon.

3. Feel free to build up the layers of papers and color until the piece looks right to you.

This project works as a great warm-up exercise to stimulate ideas for other collages, or you can make daily-life collages for their own sake. You can work on one of them intensely or make a series of five to ten quick collages.

You could expand this project to create a daily or occasional collage journal (see chapter 7), using scraps to document particular events or using those events as springboards for further creative expression. Kristen Mills kept such a journal for a year.

Jane Davies: Right Now! 9″ x 6″
My own attempt at a daily-life collage.

Ephemera Beyond the Everyday
Photos and documents can suggest subject matter that connects with you personally.

If you are lucky enough to have one, a stash of old family photographs, documents, scrapbooks, linens and lace, etc. can be a wonderful source for collage material, stimulating all kinds of ideas for subject matter that is connected with you personally. As you go through old photographs and ephemera it is a good idea to make notes about the people, places, time periods, and contexts they represent, if you have access to this information. You may find yourself collaging about an event that happened a generation or two ago that has affected your life or circumstances in some way. In order to preserve the original materials it is best to scan or photocopy them for use in collage.

Collecting other people's ephemera is fun because you can imagine the lives of the previous owners and users. Flea markets and used-book stores are excellent sources for anonymous ephemera. Look for old postcards, brochures, maps (I *love* maps!), catalogs, magazines, sheet music, dress patterns, etc. If you are buying used books for collage, look for ones with interesting typefaces or illustrations. I particularly like old dictionaries, language instruction books, and books with tables, diagrams, or maps.

Small objects
Flea-market finds and junk-drawer contents can become embellishments for collage.

Small found objects make good embellishments, accents, or focal points for collage. Buttons, charms, jewelry parts, game pieces, beads, doll parts, dried natural materials, feathers, fishing tackle, hardware of all sorts, shells, bits of wood and bone, sea glass, clock parts, and computer chips are just a few of the kinds of pieces you could use in collage. In addition to your stash of paper and ephemera, make a stash of found objects.

Magazines and Catalogs
Magazines and catalogs can be rich sources of color and texture.

Before throwing your mail-order catalogs or magazines into the recycling bin, look through them for potential collage material. Magazines and catalogs can be rich sources of color and texture. I particularly like the color swatches in the catalog sections that show the available colors for a given product. I was turned on to these by Autumn Hathaway's "Oh My!" journal page, and have experimented with them in my collage journal. Fashion magazines offer the rich colors and patterns of fabrics, skin tones, makeup, and hair, along with a two-dimensional sense of their textures. Home and garden publications offer the same in their pictures of carpets and rugs, wood grain, and wallpapers, as well as stone, brick, foliage, and other outdoor materials.

In addition to colors, patterns, and textures, magazines and catalogs are terrific sources of imagery. For figures—faces, clothing and accessories, body parts, eyes, mouths, hands, etc.—I often buy a couple of fashion magazines (besides, I get some good makeup tips and free fragrance samples). Clothing catalogs are another good source for figures. If you are looking for a particular type of imagery—boats, plants, houses, interior spaces, fish, food, etc.—consider buying an issue or two of a magazine on the topic at your local bookstore or newsstand. Artist Dawne Polis subscribes to several art and antiques magazines just for collage material.

ADHESIVES

For most collage applications, plain white glue is a perfectly serviceable adhesive. It is widely available and relatively inexpensive. This type of glue is available under many brand names—Elmer's, Sobo, and Aleene's are just a few—that vary only slightly in working properties. It dries clear and does not wash off. (Be sure when purchasing adhesives not to buy "washable" glue, which does wash off after drying.) White glue is generally not archival (acid-free), but it will last many years before showing its age.

Polyvinyl acetate, or PVA, is very similar to white glue, but it is usually archival. (Some white glues are, in fact, made from PVA, but are not archival.) Check the label if you are concerned about the longevity of your adhesive. Often you will find archival PVA in the bookbinding section of your art-supply store or catalog.

Pastes, made from plant starches such as wheat starch or methyl cellulose, are another option. They are often used in bookbinding because they are generally archival. And they are reversible— you can wash them off if you get some on your fine book cloth or hand-marbled end papers. Another advantage of pastes is that they dry flat, whereas white glue and PVA will cause lighter weight papers to curl.

Autumn Hathaway: Journal page "Oh My!"
Autumn uses color swatches from a catalog to frame her central image on this journal page, shown at top.

Jane Davies: Journal page
Inspired by Autumn, I created a journal page to try out different types of color swatches—yarns, sheets, and towels—along with some other colorful papers.

PURCHASED MATERIALS

Indulge in a few luscious papers to add color, pattern, and texture to your stash.

There is a huge variety of decorative papers available at paper stores, art-supply stores, and online. You can find papers made from many fibers with interesting textures and earthy colors; handmade papers that incorporate such natural elements as flowers and petals; screen-printed papers from all over the world; and high-tech metallic and holographic papers. I recommend indulging in a few luscious papers once in a while to augment your stash and to add color, pattern, and texture to it. Decorative art papers can be expensive, but the sheets are generally big enough for you to use them in many collages.

Colored tissue paper is a great material for creating swaths of color (see chapter 3, "Painting with Paper," for suggestions on how to use tissue paper). It is inexpensive and readily available in craft stores and often the gift-wrap section of other stores. Some tissue paper bleeds color when wetted with glue or medium, and some does not; either type can produce beautiful results. Test it on a piece of scrap paper before using it in a collage.

The scrapbooking and rubber-stamping worlds have exploded with many new, wonderful collage materials from patterned papers to unusual fibers, stickers, embellishments, hardware, words and phrases in all different forms, manufactured "found" objects (such as game pieces and Scrabble tiles), and "collage sheets" of vintage and designer imagery; many examples of such materials are available in scrapbooking and rubber-stamping stores. Clip art from books or CDs is another rich source of material available for purchase. You can indulge in these to the extent that your budget allows, but many veteran collagers feel that the most expressive collages are achieved by including imagery and materials with which you have a personal connection.

HAND-RENDERED MATERIALS

Develop your artistic identity by adding your own artwork to your collage materials.

Including hand-rendered materials, in addition to your authentic ephemera and flea-market finds, helps add a personal touch. Try saving grocery lists, to-do lists, doodles you make while on the phone, quick off-the-cuff diagrams, directions, telephone messages, old checkbook registers, etc. Play Pictionary and save the drawings! Any

mark made by hand falls into this category. You can see a fragment of Kristen Mill's grocery list at the bottom of the daily-life collage on page 14 (left).

In addition to the scrawls and scribbles of everyday life, adding your own artwork to your vocabulary of collage materials is important to developing your unique artistic identity. Finding ways to make your own materials is as important to the process as gathering and choosing found and purchased materials.

If you don't feel you have adequate drawing or painting skills, try drawing and painting with the intention of tearing up the results for collage! This is in the category of dance-like-nobody's-watching. My book Collage with Color is full of decorative painting techniques for creat-

ing patterned papers of your own. Creating paint play-grounds (see "Playing with Paint," on page 64 of this book) is a great way to awaken your inner painter as well as generate lots of gorgeous collage material.

Other techniques for creating your own collage materials include painting tissue paper (chapter 3), making gel transparencies (chapter 4), and altering materials digitally ("Digital Alterations," page 46).

Jane Davies: Doodle collage
This collage was made exclusively from my scribble drawings and "paint playgrounds."

Project:
Doodle Collage
Drawing materials offer rich possibilities for creating unique collage papers.

Making a collage out of your scribbles is a great way to free up your intuitive drawing and painting skills. This process can also produce a very vibrant and personal collage. Drawing materials offer rich possibilities for creating unique collage papers. Experiment with different combinations of crayon, charcoal, pastel, Conté crayon, oil pastel, watercolor crayons, graphite stick, regular pencils, pens of various sorts, colored pencils, oil stick, and any other materials you can draw with. For additional effects, combine these media with water, watercolor, or drawing inks.

1. Create a series of eight to ten scribble drawings on inexpensive paper using any combination of drawing materials you choose. Work quickly and spontaneously, spending less than five minutes on each sheet of paper. If you find yourself stuck or thinking too much about what to do next, stop and move onto the next drawing. Make some "paint playgrounds" (see "Playing with Paint," page 64) too, if you like. Try to get as much variety of color and mark-making style as you can with the materials you have chosen.

2. Spread these drawings and paintings out in front of you so you can look at them all at once. Cut or tear out parts that you particularly like, keeping the shapes simple. I tore my scribbles into squares and rectangles.

3. Play with your shapes on a clean background until you find a composition that you are happy with, and then glue them to the support. You may choose to glue pieces as you cut them out, building the collage intuitively, rather than deciding on the composition before committing to it.

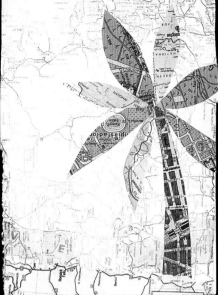

Jane Davies: Palm Trees, 7″ x 5″ each
Three different versions of my palm trees.

Project:
One Object, Ten Collages

Exploring collage materials can be a way to get started or the beginning of a series.

This project is a way to explore your collage materials freely and intuitively within the framework of a given subject. It is meant as a warm-up or a way to get started if you are stuck for ideas, but you can certainly develop it into a series, if that seems right.

1. Choose an object you would like to depict. Something simple and easily recognizable works best: a fish, a tree, a flower, a boat, a landscape, the sun, a heart, a leaf, a star, or even a figure. Anything that you feel is approachable in collage will work.

2. Start collaging. Working in a fairly small format, begin making collages depicting your chosen object. One approach is to make ten (or however many you choose) versions of one object, as I did with the palm trees. Another approach is to depict the object in varying circumstances. Vary the materials, composition, colors, backgrounds, and embellishments. Work quickly and spontaneously until you feel you are on a roll.

It is not necessary to make ten collages; the point is to explore your materials without getting hung up on any one piece. If you get stuck on a particular collage, put it aside and move on to the next one.

Autumn Hathaway: Group of ATCs, 3¹/₂˝ x 2¹/₂˝ each (standard ATC size)
Autumn used paper, fabric, buttons, beads, staples, stitching, and stamping to create this group of ATCs.

Project:
Artist Trading Cards (ATCs)

Artists make ATCs for the sheer joy of creating and sharing.

Artist trading cards, or ATCs, are 3¹/₂˝ x 2¹/₂˝ cards that artists of all media make to trade or to keep. The one rule in the ATC world is that the cards must never be sold. They are for the joy of creating and sharing. When you trade them, you should put your name and contact information somewhere on the card. It can be part of the embellishment or be written discreetly on the back.

Jane Davies: Group of ATCs
My group of ATCs all started from the same all-over collage (at right).

Jane Davies: All-over collage, 20˝ x 18˝
Unaccustomed to working in an ATC-size format, I made this all-over random collage from which I then cut 3 ½˝ x 2 ½˝ rectangles.

ATCs are fun to make as a group activity. Put some collage materials out in the middle of a table, and add glue, paper towels, watercolor crayons, colorful threads, and a stack of papers, illustration board, or cardboard, cut to the standard ATC size. Put out a little wine and cheese on a sideboard and have your pals over, whether they consider themselves artists or not. When you put a group of people together in a room with a pile of art materials, you can count on a rich exchange of ideas and a damn good time.

A few ways to make ATCs:

1. Start by cutting some paper or board into 3½˝ x 2½˝ rectangles. Then simply start collaging on them one at a time or in batches. Glue down some collage materials on each one, and then go back and add paint to or draw on the collages, or add more collage elements. Keep working the group until you feel your ATCs are done or you just want to move on. You can always come back to them later.

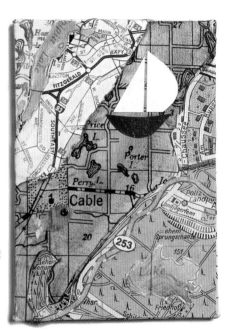

2. If you find the 3½″ x 2½″ format too small, try doing a random collage on a larger piece of paper, as in my all-over collage on page 23. Then cut a 3½″ x 2½″ viewfinder out of a piece of heavy paper and use it to find interesting compositions within the large collage. Cut out those compositions, and then add something to each one; I did this in my "Group of ATCs."

3. Instead of paper, choose some other material for your support—wood, fabric (see Autumn Hathaway's "100% Wool"), felt, leather, metal, etc. I've chosen to use foam core for some of my ATCs. I like its thickness and the ease of cutting. I start by wrapping the foam core with a piece of paper and then collage on it. The edges provide another surface for decorating.

Jane Davies: Flapper
The foam core in this ATC gave me a sturdy base around which to wrap metallic thread.

Autumn Hathaway: 100% Wool
Autumn's ATC on wool makes playful use of the tag.

Jane Davies: Gone Fishing
The boat and the fish make whimisical accents on this ATC collage of maps.

Once you have your ATCs, you can trade them with other artists, keep them and refer to them for inspiration, or exhibit them (see "Making a Foam-Core Frame for an ATC"). Go back to making them once in a while as a collage warm-up or just to play with your materials.

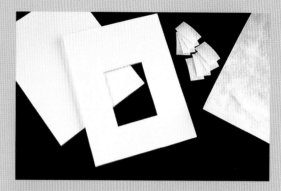

Materials for foam-core frame
1. Cut two pieces of foam core to the desired size of your frame. Cut an opening on one of them slightly bigger than your ATC. I cut mine 4″ x 3″ so there would be a quarter-inch space on all sides. Cut eight little tabs of rice paper approximately 1 ¹⁄₂″ x ¹⁄₂″.

Gluing down the corner tabs
2. Glue the rice-paper tabs to the inside corners of the opening of the foam core piece that will be the front of the frame.

Brushing glue onto the frame
3. Cut two sheets of rice paper the size of your foam core, plus 1″ of overhang on all sides. Brush glue on one side of the front piece of foam core.

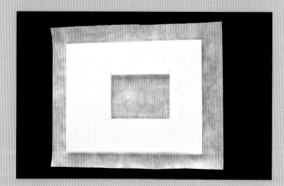

Placing the foam-core frame on the rice paper
4. Adhere it to a sheet of rice paper.

Cutting the corners
5. Cut an opening in the rice paper inside the opening of the foam core, leaving about ³⁄₄″ overhang. Cut slits diagonally from the inside corners of the foam core to the inside corners of the opening in the rice paper.

Folding up the insides of the opening

6. Brush glue on each of these tabs and wrap them around the foam-core opening.

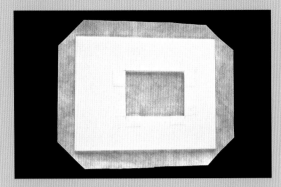

Cutting off the outside corners

7. Cut the corners off the rice paper to about ¼″ from each corner of the foam core.

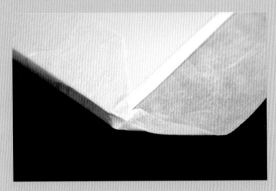

Folding up the outside corners

8. Glue and fold each side of the rice paper, making sure to tuck in the corners.

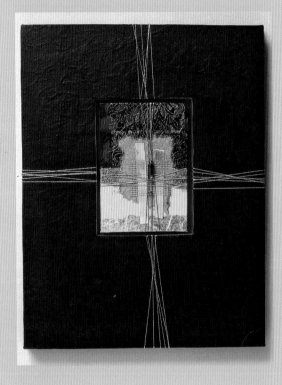

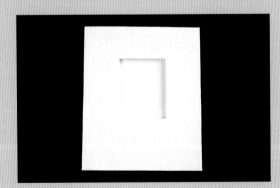

Putting the two pieces together

9. Wrap the second piece of foam core in rice paper in a similar manner (except for the opening). Put the two pieces together and you have a frame ready to paint, collage, or otherwise embellish.

Painting and embellishing

I painted and embellished my frame to become an extension of the ATC.

ORGANIZING YOUR COLLAGE MATERIALS

Some artists thrive on chaos. If you don't, organizing your materials is a good place to start.

Now you have collected and created many wonderful materials and are ready to jump in head first. But where do you start? There are almost too many choices, and it can be overwhelming. Some artists thrive on the chaos of many different materials competing for attention. However, for many others, some (at least minimal) sense of order is required. Organizing your collage materials into broad categories is a good place to start.

I find it useful to make a distinction between *imagery* and *pattern–texture–color*. We could call these categories *images* and *formal elements*. Images include any kind of pictures you use as such. (For example, if you use a picture of a red rose to add some red to an abstract composition, you are not using it as an image, but rather for its formal—in this case, color—quality). Images can come from many of the sources—photographs, drawings, rubber stamps; even decorative, patterned paper or fabric might have images on it. Formal elements, on the other hand, are materials you choose for their color, pattern, texture, quality of line, etc., rather than their imagery. These two categories will overlap in many instances, but I find it useful to think about materials in these terms and then feel free to cross categories when necessary.

GLUING TIP

Gluing with a credit card
After gluing down a collage paper, burnish it with a bone folder (a smooth tool shaped like a letter opener and used by book binders for scoring, folding, and tearing paper) or a discarded credit card to remove all the air bubbles. First lay a piece of wax paper over the glued paper, then drag the credit card or bone folder over it, similar to the way you would use a squeegee.

THE COLLAGE ARTIST'S TOOLBOX

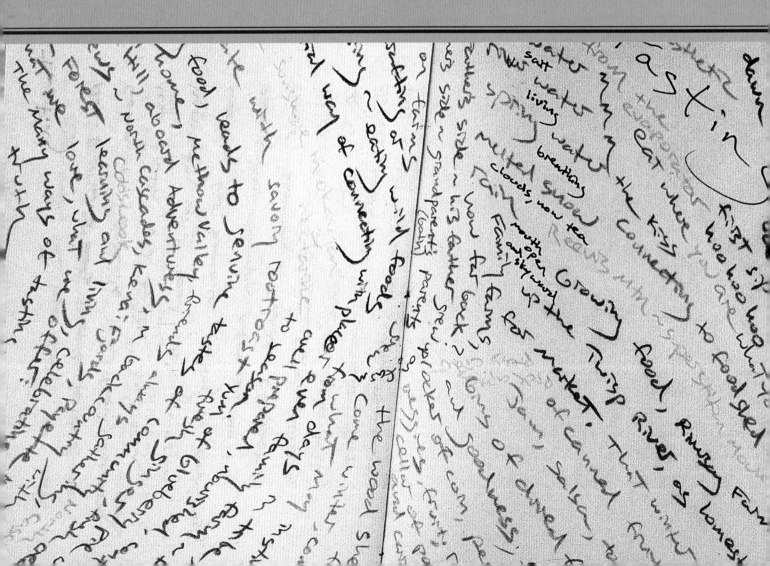

Treat your stashes like compost heaps that you keep full and occasionally turn over. Keeping ideas churning sets the stage for happy accidents, free associations, and synthesis.

The collage artist's toolbox is a set of practices that keeps the creative fire going. These include:

- Gathering and generating materials and imagery.
- Keeping your stashes—imagery, color and texture, text, small objects—full and occasionally turned over, much as you would keep a compost heap (stashes are discussed in chapter 1).
- Keeping an ongoing collage journal (as discussed in chapter 7) is another important practice, whether it is a purely visual sketchbook-style journal or one that includes written ideas and observations.

The basic idea is that you keep ideas churning in several different realms (images, words, materials, techniques, ideas) and in this way create the conditions for happy accidents, free associations, analysis, and synthesis—in other words, art.

WRITTEN JOURNAL
Begin a sketchbook-style journal or one that includes written ideas and observations.

Another practice you might add to your toolbox is keeping a written journal. This does not mean committing yourself to daily entries to keep a record of what happened on a particular day. Rather, it is an opportunity to vent, to work out something that is bothering you,

Joshua Porter: Journal page
Joshua used colored pencils to brainstorm ideas for his collage prayer flags (see page 115). The different colors express various trains of thought on a topic.

or to simply explore your feelings or ideas at the moment. Once you get used to talking to yourself on paper, journaling can be a means of unlocking your creativity and discovering what kinds of ideas and issues are important to you. Writing can be a means of "taking out the garbage" in order to let the deeper stuff surface. That is, you write down all the chit-chat that is in your head so that you can let it go and move on to more important things.

Your written journal is the place to let your ideas surface, for better or worse, and to give them breathing room, voice, and space; to put them out there for examination.

Do not attempt to write and to examine or edit at the same time. Let your thoughts share the page with other thoughts they might not have met otherwise. This is the essence of free association.

Free-Writing Exercise
Writing regularly can be a useful exercise for generating ideas.

This exercise will be familiar to many, as it is one frequently found in writing classes and instruction books. I find it the single most useful exercise for generating and articulating ideas. For this exercise, all you need is a pen and paper or a few blank journal pages. Set yourself a time limit—start with two minutes, and work up to five as you get used to it—and write constantly for that period of time. Don't stop to think, edit, evaluate, wonder what to say next, or cross anything out. Just keep writing. If you get stuck, simply repeat the last word you wrote over and over again until something else pops into your head. If you need a starting point, here are a few suggestions:

- Describe your childhood home room by room until your description triggers a specific memory. Write about the memory and see where it leads.

- Write ten to fifteen words that you would use to describe yourself. They can be nouns, verbs, or adjectives. Don't think—just write. These one-word descriptions are like hypotheses, not facts, so don't worry about being accurate. Without stopping the flow of writing, choose one of the words and elaborate on it.

- Describe how you imagine your life will be at some specific future date. This can be fantasy, reality, or some of each. I sometimes begin this exercise by placing myself very specifically in time and space. For example, I am on my sofa at eight o'clock in the morning in early October 2010.

- Write a letter to yourself at a different age. Write to your adolescent self, or to yourself as a child or an elderly person. Or write a letter to yourself at your current age from yourself at a different age.

Jane Davies: Collage journal double-page spread, 12˝ x 9˝
This collage journal double-page spread stemmed from musings about the Halifax Explosion in my written journal (see "After the Explosion," on page 117). During a free-writing session I found myself exploring places I had known as a child in Halifax, and how I remembered them.

The process of writing regularly will unleash a flow of ideas. If this free-writing exercise appeals to you, try to set aside time to do it, perhaps a few minutes every day, or at least a few times a week. Choose an inexpensive journal that is comfortable to hold, and a pen that you like to use. Or, you might prefer to do the free-writing on the computer. Whichever way suits you, try to do it as often as possible, even if it is just for two minutes at a time.

Using Your Writing to Generate Ideas for Collage
Articulating thoughts verbally can help you articulate meaning visually.

Articulating thoughts verbally can help you articulate meaning visually, and vice versa. Writing in response to visuals increases your awareness of how a collage can express ideas and emotions. Many artists use writing as a tool to help them understand their visual work. You may find it useful to write about your processes, or your responses to your own and others' artwork. However, writing is *not* visual art. It is important not to get too visual in your writing, or, rather, not to get too committed to a visual idea in writing. When I do this, here is what happens: While writing, I can *see* the visual manifestation of the idea, and it looks great in my head and "on paper." When I get out to the studio, the idea falls flat. It sounded good, but I can't make it happen in the actual materials. If your writing gets too visually descriptive, it's probably time to go to the studio and start making collage. It has taken me a while to become aware of that balance between visual expression and verbal reflection, and with practice you will find your own sense of it.

Cynthia Gregory: A Little Green, 25″ x 11″
This piece is based on color memory, which Cynthia prepared for by brainstorming in writing. The writing helped her articulate her feelings and memories associated with the color green.

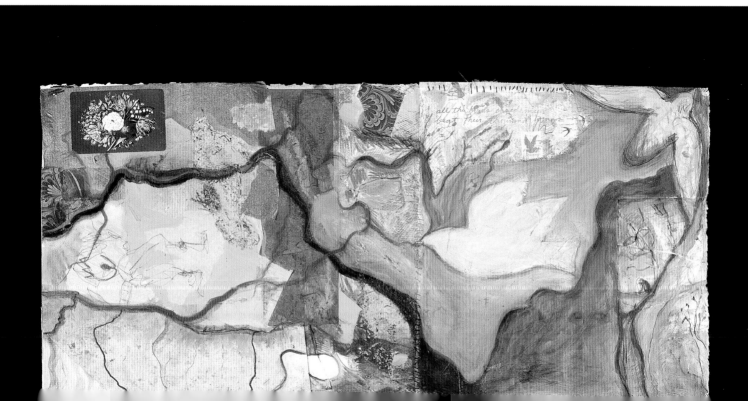

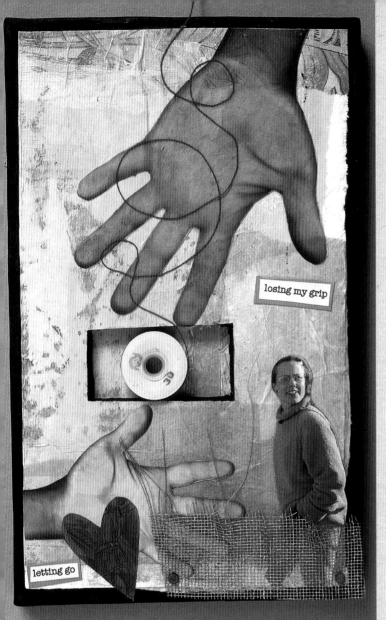

losing my grip

letting go

Jane Davies: Letting Go/Losing My Grip, 8½″ x 5½″
The title and text of this collage come directly from my idea list. It is one of several collages in which I explore this two-sided concept.

recognize as significant. When I see one of these ideas emerging, or when I find I've written a phrase that seems to have metaphoric potential, I add it to my *idea list*. The idea list is simply a list of themes, possible titles, phrases, etc., that I might want to examine in my collage work. I keep it on a separate page in my notebook, and add to it and edit it as my interests evolve. I refer to my idea list when a collage starts to reveal a theme, when I am developing a theme, or when I need a title or punch line for a piece in progress. I also refer to the idea list for a collage starting point.

From your written journal, or from out of the blue, start a list of words, phrases, and ideas that have particular resonance for you. You could just go through your journal and highlight particular phrases, but if you put them in a separate list, they may dance on the page, pair up, and free-associate in unexpected ways. Add to and revise your list periodically. My idea list includes a lot of clichés and wordplay, some image descriptions, and words or phrases that indicate subject matter I want to examine. Some of these are title-worthy, while others are just ideas I want to play with in collage. Here are a few examples from my idea list, some of which have made it into collages:

- Drawing parallels
- Unintended consequences
- Falling into place
- Boundaries (journal double-page spread "Personal Boundaries," page 77)
- Navigating the abyss
- Mood swing
- Emotional attachments

Project:
The Idea List

Add recurring themes or phrases with metaphor potential to your idea list.

I am a big fan of writing as an integral part of the creative process. It can be therapeutic as a creative activity in itself, but it can also be an effective way to generate ideas for collage. I find that writing frequently reveals recurring themes and concepts that I might not otherwise

Jane Davies: LaHave chronicles journal page
A letter from my friend Gloria, who lives in LaHave, Nova Scotia, was the inspiration for this journal page.

VISUAL VOCABULARIES

The more you work, the more certain colors, textures, and patterns become part of your visual language.

Building a vocabulary of images and materials that are particularly meaningful to you is part of growing as an artist. Certain colors, textures, and patterns become part of your personal visual language. The more you work, the more you develop your own tastes and obsessions, and a kind of personal iconography emerges. It is easy to borrow imagery from others, or to purchase it ready-made. This may be a good way to begin if you are new

to collage and need a starting point. However, as you work, you "audition" different kinds of images and materials until you find ones that suit your sense of rightness of expression. One of the reasons for creating your own collage materials (see chapter 1, page 18) is to develop your unique voice. Even if you use appropriated imagery, you will develop your own style of putting the images together in collage.

Alix Hegeler's visual vocabulary includes British tabloids; foreign newspapers; newspaper printing plates (her support material, some of which she leaves exposed); dress patterns; finely rendered drawings and paintings of pears, figures, etc.; architectural drawings; and house imagery. Each of her pieces is unique and includes materials and imagery not on this list, but all of them share much of this visual vocabulary.

Sharon McCartney's work is rich with imagery of the natural world. She uses her own watercolor paintings and drawings of birds and insects; botanical engravings; old handwritten letters; vintage linens; her own gelatin prints and sun prints; and lots of precise hand-stitching and beading. Though each piece and each series has its own unique character, these materials and the way they are put together are distinctly Sharon's.

WORKING STYLES

There is no right way of working, only your own way.

There are as many different styles of working in collage as there are collage artists. Over time, every artist develops habits and tricks of the trade—ways of working that suit his or her sensibility. There is no right way of

Alix Hegeler: Detail of panel showing some of her materials
Alix uses such diverse materials as dress patterns, architechtural plans, found text, and her own highly skilled drawing

Alix Hegeler: Detail of panel showing a unique visual vocabulary
Alix uses house imagery, architechtural plans, and newspaper printing plates as parts of her unique visual vocabulary.

working, only your own way. Some artists start their collages in a spontaneous manner, working quickly and loosely, and then agonize over the final stages of completion. Other artists don't glue anything down until they have painstakingly arranged and rearranged every piece until everything fits together as a whole. Some work on one piece at a time, while others work in groups or series. Some artists are neat and organized, while others have their own sense of organization (which may look like a disaster area to others). Time frames for working on and completing collages vary a great deal among artists. Some finish works within a sitting, while many take weeks or months to finish a group of pieces, giving them plenty of time to evolve.

I want to illustrate this point by describing my own working style and that of a few of the artists whose work appears in this book. Maybe some of these descriptions will seem familiar to you. I tend to work in quantity,

Sharon McCartney: Sincerity, 18″ x 12½″
This piece features Sharon's own drawings, vintage linens, and fine hand-stitching.

Sharon McCartney: To the Evening Star, 14½″ x 12¾″
This collage includes many of Sharon's signature elements: botanical engravings, a bird painting, handwriting, vintage linens, fine stitching, and sun prints.

starting many collages and finishing only some. I usually start by using one of the prompts listed in "spinning your wheels" (page 41) and let that begin the creative dialogue between my materials and concepts. I work on several pieces over the same period of time. Often I start a group of pieces, get partway through, and then leave them for days or weeks before returning to them while I start others. Invariably, when I get back to them I have a new perspective and bring new ideas to them. In this circuitous way, I generate a lot of collages-in-progress, and some get lost in the shuffle. I've accepted this as part of my process, and in order to make finished pieces, I also have to make a lot of unfinished pieces.

Rowena Macleod works on only a few—three or four—pieces at a time. As the pieces progress, they go through many changes. Often images don't get glued down for quite a while (perhaps weeks or months). When the pieces are "finished," Rowena hangs them on the wall to study them, and often makes changes, even at that point, because she has found better images or better ways to resolve problems she sees. Despite this long process, some works do ultimately get discarded—or back-burnered and then recycled into new works of art.

Dawne Polis usually works on pieces as individual works of art, though occasionally she works in series (as she did in the dictionary page pieces on page 95). However, she works on many individual pieces over a period of many months. Although Dawne works spontaneously, she rarely completes a piece all in one sitting. Usually it takes several months to complete one. "I have to 'live' with a piece and get to know it before I can add that finishing touch," she says. Ultimately Dawne finishes practically every piece she starts, but the occasional discard gets recycled into something new. Dawne describes herself during a collaging session:

I am a complete mess. Medium and paint all over me. Bits of scrap paper in my hair. Embossing powder on my nose. But I'm very organized with my little piles of like-minded bibelots, stashed all over, ready to be combined into a collage or assemblage when the Spirit moves.

Erika Schmidt, who is primarily a printmaker, works very methodically—meticulously cutting, arranging, and rearranging her collage elements on a spare background over a long period of time before finally committing to a particular composition and gluing the pieces in place. She has to live with them in different arrangements, often taking digital photos at different stages, before being able to see what works best.

Rowena Macleod: Two Creations, 10˝ x 8˝
Rowena depicts her life as a mother and an artist—someone who creates life and art.

Rowena Macleod: Nomad Again, 10˝ x 8˝
Rowena captures a sense of impermanence, a sad feeling of not being rooted to a place.

WORKS IN PROGRESS

When a collage looks right to you, it is finished.

How do you know when a piece is finished? How do you know when to (a) stop and call it done, (b) leave it alone and come back to it later, or (c) abandon it to the recycling bin and start over? There are no easy answers to these questions. When a collage looks right to you, it is finished. You may decide it is finished, and still come back to it later and decide to add something. Or, it may seem unfinished but you can't see how to resolve it. You have to trust your sense of what looks right, what feels resolved. The more you work, the more the answers to these questions will become clear. However, if you find yourself easily finishing every piece you start, you may want to challenge yourself to step out of your comfort zone and take more risks.

Getting Feedback

A fresh pair of eyes may see something that is not apparent to you.

If you are not sure where a piece should go next—you know it needs *something* but are not sure what—or if you can't decide whether it is finished, it is sometimes helpful to ask another person to look at it. A fresh pair of eyes may see something that is not apparent to you.

Some artists form groups that meet regularly to talk about each other's work. This can be extremely constructive, motivating, and inspiring, but it may not be practical for everybody. I find it helpful to invite another artist over to my studio once in a while, either to work together or to have her or him look at my work. And occasionally I go to another artist's studio to look at her or his work. For me, this informal, one-on-one format is more workable than a regular group meeting. Either way, convening with other artists can be a vital part of your creative life.

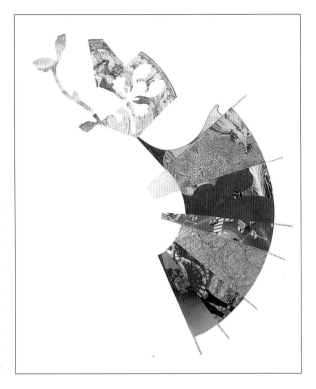

Erika Schmidt: From her "Unfolding" series, 40″ x 26″
Erika's work has a clean precise look, achieved only after many rearrangements of collage elements.

It is important to give and take feedback with a non-evaluative, inquiring attitude. You don't need someone else to tell you whether your work is "good" or "bad," but it is helpful to share insights and responses to each other's work, or to make suggestions when asked. You can be on the verge of giving up on a piece and relegating it to the recycling bin, when another artist looks at it and sees great possibility. Sometimes his or her insights will inspire you to continue working on the piece—and sometimes not. Listen to your own inner voice, but at the same time be open to another's suggestions. You don't want to end up finishing a collage the precise way that someone else suggested, just to please him or her. Whether or not you choose to take someone else's suggestions, another view can help you see your work in a different way and open your eyes to new possibilities.

Jane Davies: Small study I. 6˝ x 4 1/2˝
Jane Davies: Small study II. 6 1/2˝ x 4 3/4˝
Jane Davies: Small study III. 6˝ x 4 1/2˝
I created these pieces by playing with scraps on small supports cut from discarded collages.

WORKING OUTSIDE YOUR COMFORT ZONE
To grow as a collage artist you must move out of your comfort zone. Use your written journal to identify areas where you want to challenge yourself.

It is important to develop a rapport with your materials, techniques, and concept vocabularies. However, to grow as a collage artist you must move out of your comfort zone. Consider the following challenges:

- **Material.** Introduce a material you've never used. For example, if you never use fabric, collect scraps in various weights and textures, and try a series of small collages featuring them, along with other, more familiar materials.

radically different scale. I work most comfortably at 5˝ x 4˝ or 12˝ x 9˝, so creating ATCs at 3 1/2˝ x 2 1/2˝ was a challenge, and I occasionally work on 30˝ x 22˝ sheets of watercolor paper.

- **Format.** If you generally create collages in one format (say, on a flat sheet of paper), try a different one. The difference between paper and stretched canvas, with its texture and thickness, can inspire a new way of thinking about collage. As a further challenge, try a three-dimensional construction or an accordion book format. If you always work in your collage journal, make some collages outside your journal. (See chapter 6 for a discussion of format.)

- **Painting and drawing.** Try using paint in ways that are unfamiliar to you (see "Playing with Paint," page 64), or experiment with a paint type you haven't used before. Try a doodling exercise (see page 20) with a few new drawing tools, then incorporate them into a collage.

- **Imagery.** Try new imagery. If you regularly use figures or faces in your work, try collages without them. Choose another kind of imagery, or make collages that are non-representational. Create images in unfamiliar ways (see chapter 4).

- **Color.** Gather papers, paint, and drawing materials in your least favorite colors or colors you almost never use, and make a series

Use your written journal to identify areas where you want to challenge yourself. Studying a group of your collages and recording their shared characteristics—size, format, painting and drawing, imagery, color, and other categories—will suggest ways to challenge yourself and give you insight into your visual vocabulary.

Generally, you can make revisions throughout the collaging process. If you don't like a glued-down element, you can glue something over it or cover it with gesso. Still, sometimes you go past a point of no return and your collage looks too cluttered or overworked. Even experienced artists occasionally keep adding to a piece past the point where it would have been finished. When this happens, put the piece aside and come back to it later. You may be able to use pieces of it in future collages. Sometimes I scan a failed collage from my recycling bin, then cut it into small pieces—5˝ x 4˝ or ATC size, 3 $\frac{1}{2}$˝ x 2 $\frac{1}{2}$˝— and play with them as Collage-a-Day projects (see page 43). Making digital alterations to the scan can generate more collage material (see

Jane Davies: Small playing-with-scraps collages, roughly 6˝ x 4 $\frac{1}{2}$˝ each
I scanned and digitally altered discarded collages from my recycling bin, then used them as supports for these two pieces.

KEEPING UP THE MOMENTUM

To get a fresh start when you feel blocked, go through your stashes or gather new materials.

Creative Blocks and Bottlenecks

Everyone feels uninspired or stuck once in a while and has a hard time moving forward creatively. Sometimes I get stuck because I simply feel empty of ideas, as if my creative well has run dry. In this uninspired state, even if I have some partial ideas in my head or on paper they can all fall flat once I get to the studio and try to make something. This is a creative block. One way to get a fresh start when you are feeling blocked is to go through your stashes of materials or to gather new materials. Look through books and magazines for inspiration from other artists, or try some new techniques and put the samples in your hand-rendered materials stash. Some people, notably Julia Cameron in her book *The Artist's Way*, call this "filling the well."

At other times I feel I have so many ideas competing for my attention that none of them seems any more compelling than the others and it is hard to focus. I call this a creative bottleneck. All of the ideas get stuck at the point between thinking and doing, so none of them emerges with any clarity. It is as if I am on idea overload, and the whole creative works gets jammed up. One remedy for a creative bottleneck is simply to prioritize, set some parameters for a project, and start there. The other ideas creating the bottleneck may all fall by the wayside, but if I don't act on one of them, then *all* of the ideas that once seemed equally compelling fall flat and lose their appeal. When you are frustrated by a creative bottleneck, your first attempt at a project may not immediately inspire you. Work at it a bit, and if you are still not feeling in the groove, then move onto the next one.

Another approach to dealing with a creative bottleneck is to use a collage journal (see chapter 7) to get all the ideas out. For each of your ideas, create a brainstorming page or double-page spread. Make notes and sketches and attach samples of materials you'd like to use in each project. For some of your ideas, the journal page may be enough. In other cases your collage journaling will lead you to more substantial projects.

Spinning Your Wheels as Part of the Process

When you feel uninspired, engaging with materials lets your creative faculties free-associate.

It is important to observe your creative ebb and flow. When your creativity is on the ebb, what can you do to

Autumn Hathaway: Journal double-page spread of pieces made by playing with scraps
Playing with her scraps on six 3″ x 5″ index cards, Autumn put them in a journal double-page spread.

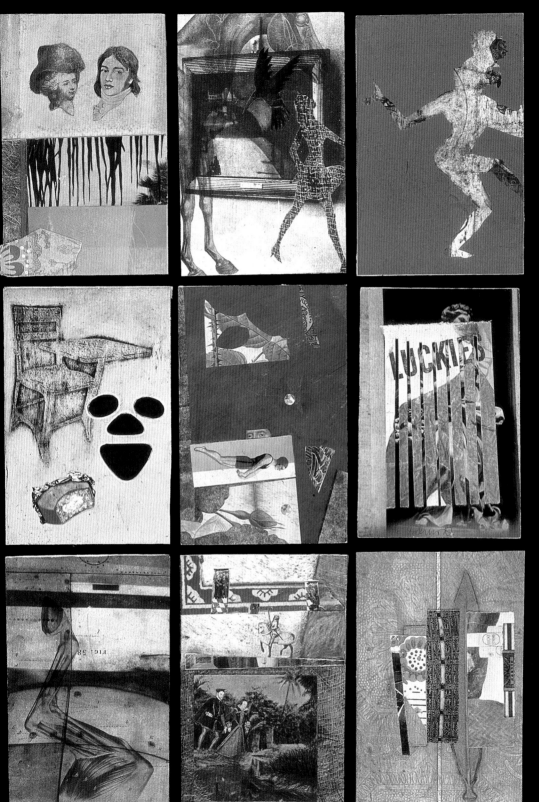

nudge it back to the flow? One thing that helps me is to have some "busy work" that keeps my hands occupied but does not demand too much inspiration. The only way to get beyond a block or a bottleneck is to do *something*, even if it feels like you are just spinning your wheels.

When your art-making feels dull or uninspired, the simple act of engagement with your materials gives your creative faculties practice in free-associating and your hands some practice in technique. Spinning your wheels is part of the process of making art, just as practicing scales is part of making music.

Here are some suggestions for projects, some described in other chapters, that you can do to spin your wheels when you are not feeling inspired.

- Make some hand-rendered collage materials as described in chapter 1, or use your photo-editing software to make multiple versions of materials you already have (see "Digital Alterations," page 46).
- Make some ATCs (described in chapter 1).
- Take out your color stashes and make some color collages as described on page 51 and 52.
- Create backgrounds as described in chapter 4. Random collage backgrounds are a fun way to get started. You can choose what to do with them later when you are feeling more inspired.
- Create a fairly large, all-over collage, as described in chapter 1, and cut it into pieces to be used later as backgrounds for new collages.
- Try layering and excavating, as described in chapter 4, using random materials. Consider these as starts for future collages.

Erika Schmidt: "Wish You Were Here" postcard collages, 6″ x 4″ each
Erika played with her scraps on this series of postcard-size collages.

- Create text using any of the techniques described in chapter 5.
- Do the Word-Image Association exercise on page 100.
- Start a new double-page spread in your collage journal, or work on a page in progress (see chapter 7).
- Make some random unbound collaged folios as described in chapter 7. Put them together to create a book.
- Play with your scraps. When I clean off my worktable for a fresh start (which happens only every couple of weeks), I keep the tiny scraps of collage materials together in one stash. Playing with these little bits and pieces in a small format (5″ x 4″ or smaller) often draws me into my creative zone. (See my small studies on page 39.)
- Rescue some unfinished or overdone collages from your collage recycling bin and scan them. Then use your photo-editing software to create new versions of them to use as collage material (see "Digital Alterations," page 46, and my small collages on page 40).

The Collage-a-Day Project

Making art every-single-day-no-matter-what may keep your creative fire going. Doing a collage once a day is a starting point, a source of inspiration, a safe place to play.

This is not so much a single project as an ongoing practice. Some artists find that the discipline of making art every-single-day-no-matter-what is exactly the challenge they need to keep the creative fire going. For these people, this steady practice eventually becomes a welcome necessity, like daily exercise, or a habit, like brushing your teeth. For others, the pressure of having to create a collage every day is enough to kill the creative spirit. The collage-a-day may seem more like an obligation than an opportunity to be creative. For people in this camp, we'll call it collage-every-once-in-a-while. Either way, the point is to make collage as frequently as possible in a format that you find comfortable.

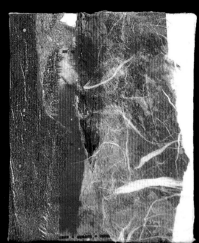
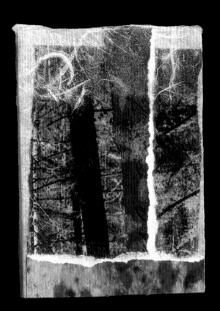
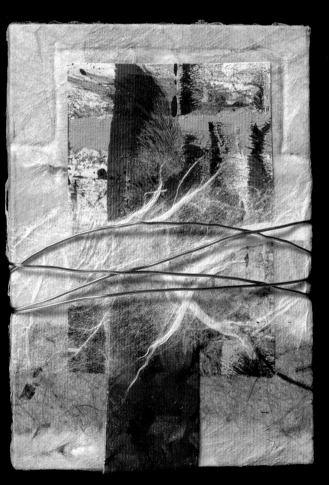
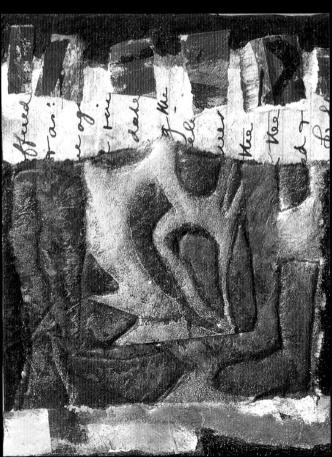

Jane Davies: Small foam-core collages, approx. 2″ x 2″ to 3″ x 2″
In three examples of my collage-a-day project, I wrapped small foam-core rectangles in paper, then used them as collage supports.

Jane Davies: Small foam-core collage with wire wrapping, 3 1/2″ x 2 1/2″
The foam core is sturdy enough to withstand heavy embellishment, such as the wire wrapping.

Jane Davies: Small foam-core collage, 5″ x 4″
I emphasized some of the lines in this collage by embossing them with a knitting needle, in the process giving the collage a quilted appearance.

You can make a commitment to yourself about the frequency and duration of your collage-a-day project—say, a collage every day for a year, or a collage once a week for six months—but you don't have to. This project is about finding a format that you become comfortable and familiar with so that it becomes a starting point, a source of inspiration, your muse, your comfy old shoes. This project gives you a safe place to play.

First, choose a format in which you can make a collage fairly quickly, and one that you find easy and inviting. The format can be a size—like an ATC—or include structural or material parameters as well: you could use a simple pamphlet book as your format, or a paper doll, or a foam-core rectangle. It can also be a page or part of a page in your collage journal. I've chosen a small (though not a specific size) foam-core rectangle as my format. I begin by wrapping it in paper; from that point on any materials or processes become fair game.

My other favorite format for this ongoing project is discarded collages cut into approximately 5″ x 4″ rectangles. I use these for backgrounds on which to play with scraps. Whatever format you choose, keep easily accessible all the materials you need for your daily collage. I keep a box of small foam-core rectangles handy, along with my four-by-fives (as I call my small rectangles of discarded collages) and scraps of collage paper. Of course, you may add other materials, but keep the basics all together.

Autumn Hathaway: Collage-a-day envelopes
Autumn uses ordinary, business-size envelopes for her collage-a-day project. She makes sure they are mail-worthy and uses them to send notes to friends. What a treat to receive one of these in the mail!

DIGITAL ALTERATIONS

Though some artists are dedicated to using all original materials, for many, computer and printing technology is an integral part of the art-making process. Using your scanner and photo-editing software can help you get the most mileage out of your artwork, photographs, and found imagery by making it possible to alter them and produce multiples.

This is not a crash course in digital imaging; it is intended for those of you who are already familiar with your scanner and photo-editing software.

Jane Davies: Collage sheet, 11˝ x 8 ¹/₂˝
I made this collage sheet with decorative paper, a corner
of a quilted jacket, a map, and a soap label.

Jane Davies: Collage sheet, 11˝ x 8 ¹/₂˝
This collage sheet includes some magazine imagery, decorative
paper, and a paper doily.

Collage sheet of small objects, using the scanner as a camera
This is a collage sheet of small objects placed directly on the scanning bed.

ADVANTAGES OF SCANNING MATERIALS

The obvious advantage to scanning your materials is that you can generate new materials by digitally altering them, creating multiple versions. Even without digital alterations, there are many advantages to scanning materials for use in collage.

- You can use an image repeatedly, trying it out in different contexts, simply by printing out multiple copies.
- If you want to preserve the original materials, such as maps, photographs, or images in books, scan them and use the printouts in your collages.
- To make your own collage sheets: Find some imagery you want to use repeatedly—vintage postcards, fabrics, wallpaper samples, your own hand-painted papers or scribble drawings (see chapter 1), magazine images, your child's drawing, a newspaper clipping, etc. Assemble the materials on the scanning bed and scan them. This is a fun way to generate a lot of material quickly without having to commit it to ink and paper. Just print out your sheets as needed.
- Use your scanner as a camera: Place objects directly on the scanning bed, drape with dark fabric, and scan. The sage leaves in "Simplicity" (page 13), and the orange slice and autumn leaves on my journal page (page 17) were created in this manner. For "Palm Reading" (page 101) I scanned my hand. Experiment with all kinds of materials, such as ribbons, textured fabrics, pebbles, wood, coins, hardware, knitted items, your hair, jewelry, keys, paper clips, etc.

- You may choose to scan original artwork in order to produce an image as an ink-jet print. This is necessary for transferring an image using acrylic medium or gel (see pages 58 and 86), or for making a gel transparency (page 89). Another reason you may prefer to use an ink-jet print is that some art materials, such as oil pastel, oil stick, and wax crayons, are resistant to glue. If you want to use such a piece of artwork in your collage, you may consider scanning it and using the printout instead.

- You can create a visual record of a collage's progress by scanning it at different stages of the process. This is an interesting exercise in its own right, but it also gives you the opportunity to experiment with taking a collage in several different directions. Print out a few copies of your piece at a given stage. Work directly on the printouts to try different ways of finishing the collage. You may adhere the printouts to a heavier sheet of paper and coat them with matte medium for stability.

- Once an image is scanned, you can print it out on any of a variety of available materials (see "Printing," page 48).

(below, left) A collage in progress, scanned
I scanned this collage while it was in progress and selected several portions to enlarge.

(below, center and right) Enlargements of selected portions of the collage in progress at left
Here are two portions I selected and enlarged to about twice their original size.

Resizing

- Select a portion of your image or pattern. In Photoshop this can be done by duplicating the image (Image ▸ Duplicate), and then cropping it using the cropping tool. Enlarge the selected portion substantially so that it becomes an abstract texture or pattern. Do this with your own painted and hand-rendered materials to generate even more unique materials. You can produce many interesting textures this way. Enlarged text is particularly interesting, especially if you can see only partial words. Enlarged maps suggest a kind of on-the-ground intimacy with the territory that is depicted.

- Scan an image or even a finished collage, and reduce the size significantly. Then use it as an element in a new collage. You can create complex collages on a small scale this way (see "Viewing," page 48). You can also reduce the size of type or handwriting to the point where it is no longer legible—transforming it into a texture or pattern—or scan and reduce purchased or handmade patterned papers to generate more variety.

- For certain types of collage projects you may need your collage elements to fit together in some way. For example, for a collage self-portrait (a journaling idea described in chapter 7), you might want to use an image of hands, but the one you have is twice as big as your original head photograph. In this case, scanning your hand image and reducing the size is an easy answer. However, part of what makes collage fresh is the juxtaposition of disparate elements of different scales. Don't be too quick to use digital resizing as a quick fix, or you might miss an opportunity to come up with a more creative solution.

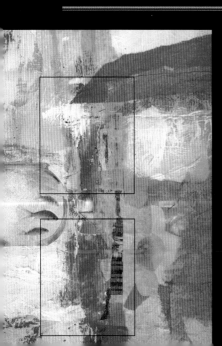

Here are some specific directions for using Photoshop.

- Desaturate your image to make it black and white: Image ◗ Adjustments ◗ Desaturate. This is a good way to make contemporary color photographs look as if they come from a different era. It gives them a veil of mystery. Once you have your black-and-white image, you can play with the brightness and contrast until it is to your liking: Image ◗ Adjustments ◗ Brightness and Contrast. Dawne Polis uses this technique.
- If you would like to make your image monochrome, go to Hue/Saturation under Adjustments in the Image menu. Click on "Colorize," and then play with the hue, saturation, and lightness sliders in the window. This is a great way to make materials for your color stashes. (See my photograph with digitally altered color, page 49.)
- Use the Hue/Saturation sliders to experiment with the color of a scanned image without "colorizing" it. Remember, you can duplicate the image (Image ◗ Duplicate) as many times as you like to make multiple versions.

PRINTING

There are papers of many different weights, textures, and materials available that are compatible with ink-jet printers. Not only are there photo papers of various qualities and surfaces, but there are also fabrics, such as cotton and organza, and translucent materials such as printable vellum and clear plastic (see the variety of transparent materials shown in the photo on page 87). In addition to papers that are made especially for your ink-jet printer, you can experiment with other kinds of paper as long as you cut them to the correct size. I've found a few kinds of almost tissue-weight sumi papers that are printer-compatible and that produce translucent printouts. Colored, patterned, printed, or textured papers can produce interesting results as well.

Jane Davies: Viewing, 7˝ x 5˝
I used a reduced version of a journal double-page spread (see page 17) as the focal point for this new collage.

Dawne Polis: Dictionary Page series, digitally altered
Dawne scanned a collage from her series and altered the color.
The resulting image has a different feel. Dawne sometimes alters
images to generate ideas for new collages.

Jane Davies: Photograph with digitally altered color
This photograph was originally taken in color. I digitally altered
it into a black-and-white image and several monochromes.

PAINTING WITH PAPER

Make a color collage as a warm-up or as a way to free youself to explore imagery.

At the end of chapter 1, we discussed organizing your collage materials into *images* and *formal elements*. Keep your organizational categories loose, so your ideas stay loose, leaving room for lots of free association, the fun part of collage. In this chapter we will make use of your non-imagery materials—materials you have collected for their color, texture, pattern, and other formal qualities.

COLOR STASHES

For the projects in this chapter, it will be useful to organize your materials in terms of color. Many of the materials we discussed in chapter 1 will apply here as well. Get a shallow box or a file folder for each color or color grouping. If you like, include a stash for neutral colors such as earth tones, beige, tan, brown, gray, and black.

Color stash of reds
Color stash of blues

You can be as broad or as narrow as you like in your color categories. For example, you could have one file for all blues, or you could have one for blue-green (warm blues) and one for blues that tend toward violet (cool blues). Or, you could go broader than that in your categorization and include all blues and purples in one stash. My reds include deep burgundies and magentas, though you could have separate files for these. I happened to find enough materials that had both pink and orange in them, so I made a separate file for pink-and-orange. There will be some overlap in your color categories, but remember to keep them loose and flexible.

I made these my stashes by first going through magazines and catalogs, cutting out samples of colors. Then I went through my collection of decorative paper samples and added some of those. I always keep colored tissue paper on hand, so for the projects in this chapter I added samples of those to my files as well. You can also include ribbons and embellishments, such as buttons and beads, to your color stashes.

Project:
Color Collage

This project involves making a collage or series of collages from a variety of materials in one color group. Leaving color choices out of the equation allows you to focus on texture, variety, composition, and imagery. This project can be used as a warm-up exercise or as a way to explore particular imagery. The basic process is that you choose a color grouping (for example, greens or reds) and make one or a series of collages using only materials in that grouping.

One approach is to choose an object or an image that is the color you have chosen—say, a tree or plant for green or a seascape for blue—and depict that object (see Melissa Patterson's color collage in green, above). Another approach is to simply make an abstract or geometric composition from your materials. Yet another way to begin is to choose as the focal point an image from your stash and build the collage around that.

Melissa Patterson: Color collage in green, 7 7/10˝ x 5 1/2˝
Melissa used papers from her green color stash to create this tree collage.

Jane Davies: Geometric color collage in blue, 10˝ x 7˝
I used images from catalogs, magazines, and discarded books, as well as decorative papers, for this geometric study of the color blue.

Jane Davies: Wild Hop, 7 1/2˝ x 5 1/2˝
A beer label inspired this color collage of amber, tan, and other neutrals.

Amanda Smith: Color collage in purple, 5 1/2˝ x 3 1/2˝
Mandy made this quilt-like color collage in purples and violets.

Jane Davies: Color collage in red and orange, 7 1/2˝ x 5 1/2˝
I used the image of a tangelo in this red-orange collage.

Jane Davies: Patchwork quilt-like geometric color collage in red, 7 1/2˝ x 5 1/2˝
Instead of making an image, you can use a color collage project to explore geometric compositions.

the elements arranged symmetrically? Does one catch the eye, or are there several elements demanding equal attention? Is your image self-contained or part of a larger composition?

A composition that "hangs together" or "looks right" is often called "unified." A composition exhibits unity when the elements relate to one another in a way that makes the composition a whole, instead of merely a collection of parts. A composition that lacks unity looks like a random jumble. The sense of what "looks right" is largely subjective, of course, but a few basic principles of composition can help you articulate your own sense of unity.

take notice of whether your collage needs a focal point or works better without one.

⦿ Choose supporting elements, not competing ones: If you do have a central image, a focal point, then try to have the other elements enhance it rather than compete with it. Again, this is a matter of personal judgment, not a hard and fast rule.

⦿ Use variety: A collage can look static or boring if all the elements are similar in size, color, or shape. If your collage is suffering from a lack of spark, try adding elements that contrast in these respects.

Jane Davies: ATCs
These three pieces are from a series of foam-core ATCs I created to explore the compositional possibilities of a set of shapes and materials.

COLLAGING OVER A PAINTED BACKGROUND
Establish a basic composition with underpainting, then fill in with color and imagery.

One approach to painting with paper is to establish a basic composition with an underpainting done in watercolor or acrylic wash. Then proceed to "fill in" the color areas or imagery with collage materials from your color groupings as well as imagery from any of your collage stashes. This is basically how Rowena McLeod begins her beautiful collages, several of which are included in this book. Rowena then draws or paints into her collages using watercolor crayons. As she builds up many layers of collage and crayon, her images change and evolve in such a way that the original composition may be completely forgotten.

In addition to a basic underpainting composition, Rowena often begins with a general concept or theme for her collage. As the piece evolves, the concept starts to take shape and become more focused. Both the concept and the composition evolve and morph continually throughout the process of layering color, image, painting, and paper. For Rowena, it is this process that is most compelling. She says her pieces almost never seem finished to her; she can always see ways of continuing. Somehow, though, Rowena brings a unity and wholeness to her pieces.

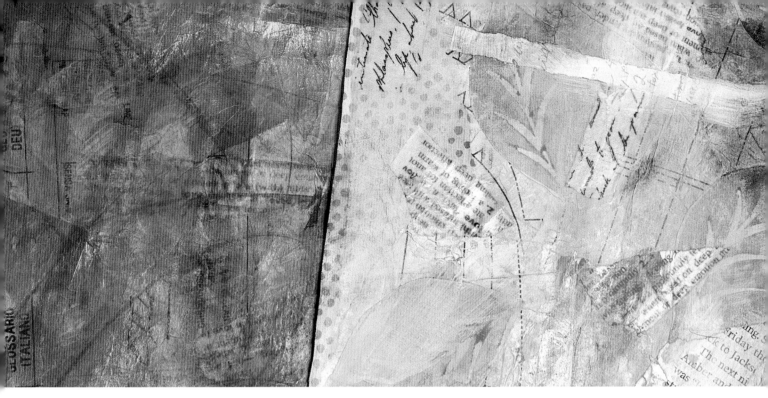

Color Sheets

Create a color sheet to build a composition or to establish a background for collage.

Color sheets are composed of layered materials in one color grouping. For the samples above I used patterned cotton fabric for the foundation, but you could as easily use a light- or medium-weight paper that is white, patterned, or a solid color. To create a color sheet you need:

- Foundation paper or fabric in your chosen color grouping (or white)
- Tissue paper and collage papers in your color grouping
- PVA glue mixed with water in a ratio of about 2:1
- Freezer paper to protect your worktable
- Acrylic paint, drawing materials, powdered pigments, or other embellishing media (optional)

1. After covering your worktable with freezer paper, brush your foundation paper or fabric with the diluted glue, and apply strips of tissue paper in the color grouping of your choice.

Color sheets

These color sheets were created by layering tissue papers and collage papers in color groups.

2. Add another application of glue, then add more papers—either colored tissue papers, or bits and fragments of collage papers or fabrics.
3. Continue to layer papers and diluted glue applications until you are satisfied with the result. Let dry overnight.
4. Once the color sheet is dry or almost dry, you can further enhance it with acrylic paint, glaze, glitter, crayon or pastel, or pearlescent pigments, as I did on the purplish sheet in the tissue papers shown above.

You can use this same process to build a collage composition or to create a background for collage. I make color sheets to use as collage material, not as collages in themselves. While working on them, I aim for an overall effect and don't think about composition.

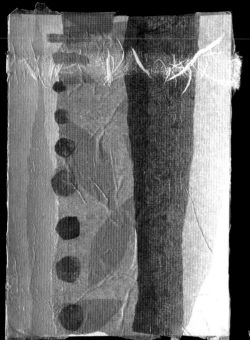

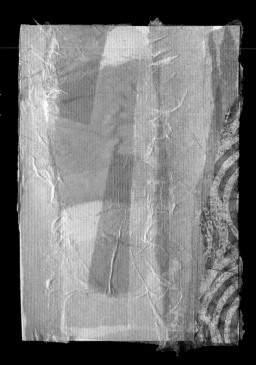

Jane Davies: Tissue-paper collage examples, 7˝ x 5˝ each
I used embellished as well as plain tissue papers in these collage studies.

Project:
Tissue-Paper Collage

**Play with colors and shapes for their own sake.
If you're getting too serious, tap into your innate
sense of play.**

This project gives you a chance to play with colors and shapes for their own sake. You probably remember making collage with tissue paper as a child. The overlapping papers create new colors and shapes on account of their translucence. If you find yourself getting too serious or bogged down with a collage, it can be helpful to take a break and tap into your innate sense of play with this exercise.

I've described this project in terms of a series of small collages, but you may choose to work in a larger format or work on only one or two pieces rather than four to eight.

1. Choose three or four colors of tissue paper, plus white or off-white translucent paper. I used white unryu, which has a characteristic long fiber texture. Cut four to eight sheets of paper, board, fabric, or other support to your desired size. I made my tissue paper collages 7˝ x 5˝. Cover your worktable with freezer paper. Cut and tear your collage papers into a variety of shapes and sizes.

2. Brush your support with matte medium and start collaging papers down, placing each piece on the support and then brushing matte medium over the top of it before continuing onto the next one.

3. Work quickly on one piece and then move onto the next, until you have made a start on each collage. Then go back and make additions to each one until you are satisfied with the compositions. I suggest working on these as a group, but if creating them one at a time makes more sense to you, then by all means do so.

EMBELLISHING TISSUE PAPER

Use painted and embellished tissue papers with abandon.

In the photo, the tissue papers were embellished with the following techniques (clockwise from the lower left):

- Lavender. I cut the leaf shapes out of lavender tissue paper and scattered them over a sheet of white tissue paper coated in matte medium. (If working on a large sheet, do this in sections so the medium doesn't dry before you place your tissue paper shapes.) I then brushed the whole surface with matte medium and laid down a sheet of lavender tissue paper. The leaf shapes are sandwiched between the lavender and the white papers.
- Green. I stamped white acrylic paint onto a sheet of green tissue paper. When the paint was dry, I coated the paper with matte medium and laid down a sheet of yellow tissue paper.
  Plum. On this sheet of plum tissue paper I simply used a rubber stamp to apply the pattern in gold metallic ink.
- Magenta. This magenta tissue paper is the kind whose color bleeds. I spritzed it with water and let it dry.
- Pink. First, I scrunched up a sheet of pink tissue paper until it was full of wrinkles. Second, I applied matte medium to a sheet of drawing paper, and then laid the tissue paper over it. I used a brayer to press all the wrinkles flat (first cover it with a sheet of wax paper).
- Black. I applied white acrylic paint to a sheet of bubble wrap, using a sponge, and then pressed the bubble wrap onto the black tissue paper.
- Turquoise. This sheet is embellished with crayon scribbles.
- Orange-Yellow. The sheet is made like the lavender leaf pattern, except I used pink and coral torn tissue-paper shapes sandwiched between a yellow sheet and an orange sheet.

At the experimental stage, don't spend too much time on each piece. You want to feel free to use your painted and embellished tissue papers with abandon. Once you feel comfortable with the process, you may want to develop more intricate tissue-paper materials.

Embellished tissue papers.
A few examples of embellished tissue paper.

ACRYLIC MEDIUMS

Acrylic mediums are like acrylic paints, but without the pigments or opacity. They dry clear, are permanent, and can't be reconstituted with water. Acrylic mediums are often mixed with acrylic paints to give them more translucence, alter their viscosity, or impart a particular sheen (matte or gloss). However, they can also be used like a decoupage medium—as an adhesive and a sealer.

Two basic types of acrylic mediums can be used this way: medium and gel. ("Medium" is the general category for clear acrylic polymer emulsions, including low-viscosity medium, high-viscosity gel, and all manner of texture mediums. "Medium" is also the term used for the lower-viscosity type of acrylic polymer emulsion.) The difference between the product called "medium" and the product called "gel" is their viscosity. Medium is more or less the viscosity of caramel sauce—thick, but pourable. Gels are like heavy-bodied acrylic paints; they have a high viscosity and hold their shape.

Both mediums and gels come in *matte* or *gloss* finishes. Matte medium is the best choice for most decoupage-like applications with lightweight papers, such as tissue paper, unryu, or lightweight ephemera. If you build up many coats of matte medium, it will begin to lose clarity and become milky. In such a case it is better to use gloss medium, which holds its clarity through many coats. If you want a matte finish, simply apply a final coat of matte medium to the finished collage.

Acrylic gel is basically the same as medium, but with a heavier body. As an adhesive, it can be used for heavier papers and even for embellishments. Used as a decoupage medium, gloss gel applied in many layers between collage elements can result in a surface of unusual depth and clarity.

Jane Davies: Nude Blues, 11″ x 9″
This is my version of Henri Matisse's
Blue Nude.

then cut out the pieces and used them as a pattern to cut out identical pieces from my own blue color sheet.

1. Find a flat image that appeals to you. Matisse cut-paper collages, quilting and appliqué designs, and clip-art designs are all good sources of flat imagery. As an alternative, you could create your own image using flat shapes. If you are using someone else's artwork, make sure that it is solely for this technique exercise or for personal exploration. Do not sell as your own a piece that has been derived substantially from someone else's work.

2. Scan the image and size it appropriately for your support.

3. Cut out the shapes and use them as templates for cutting shapes out of your collage papers.

4. Create a background using any of the techniques suggested in chapter 4. Arrange your shapes on the background and glue them down. At this point you may consider your collage finished, or you may choose to add more elements. These could be collage papers, drawing or painting, sewing, or embellishments.

Project:
Cut-Paper Collage

Cutting out abstract shapes can be a meditative way to explore composition and color.

I have always loved Matisse's cut-paper collages and decided to use them as the inspiration for playing with color sheets, tissue paper, and paint. I was unsure how to go about making a Matisse-like image on my own (they are deceptively simple-looking), so I scanned and enlarged an image from a book of one of his *Blue Nude* collages. I

Another approach is to cut abstract and geometrical shapes out of your collage papers. Cut as many shapes as you like, varying the size and using several different materials. As with the tissue-paper collage project, you can create a number of backgrounds in a small format, but you may more comfortable working on one piece at a time or in a larger format. Experiment with different arrangements of shapes on the backgrounds. When you have compositions you are happy with, glue down the pieces and embellish further, if you like. This is a meditative way to explore composition and color, or to try different combinations of materials in a simple format.

Stage 1 of background for "Nude Blues"
I created a random collage background using various kinds of found text.

Stage 2 background for "Nude Blues," with acrylic glazes added
Then I applied layers of various acrylic glazes with a sponge, wiping and blotting them in between to build up the color gradually. I added a piece of transparent unryu paper across the bottom portion.

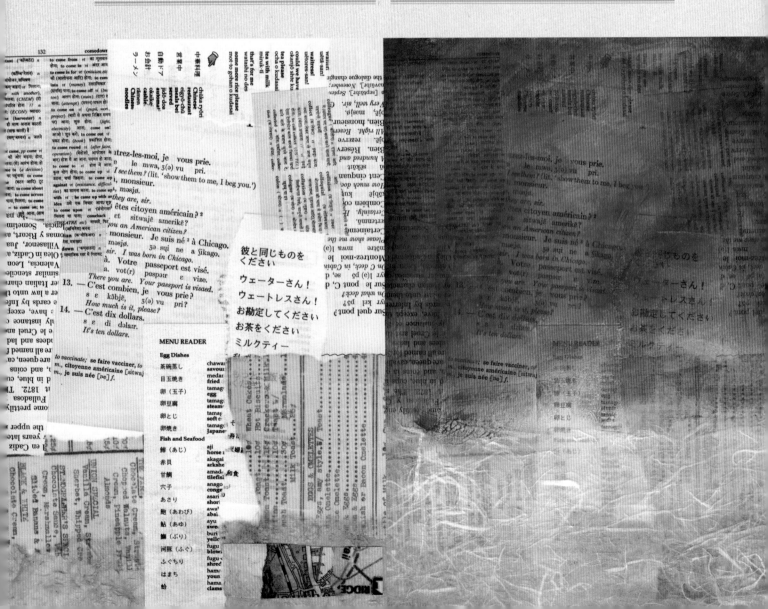

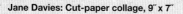

Jane Davies: Cut-paper collage, 9˝ x 7˝
I embellished this cut-paper collage with gold metallic thread,
rolled papers, and a bronze bead.

**Erika Schmidt. Two images from her "Unfolding" series,
40˝ x 26˝ each**
Erika uses the cut-paper method on a large, spare background.

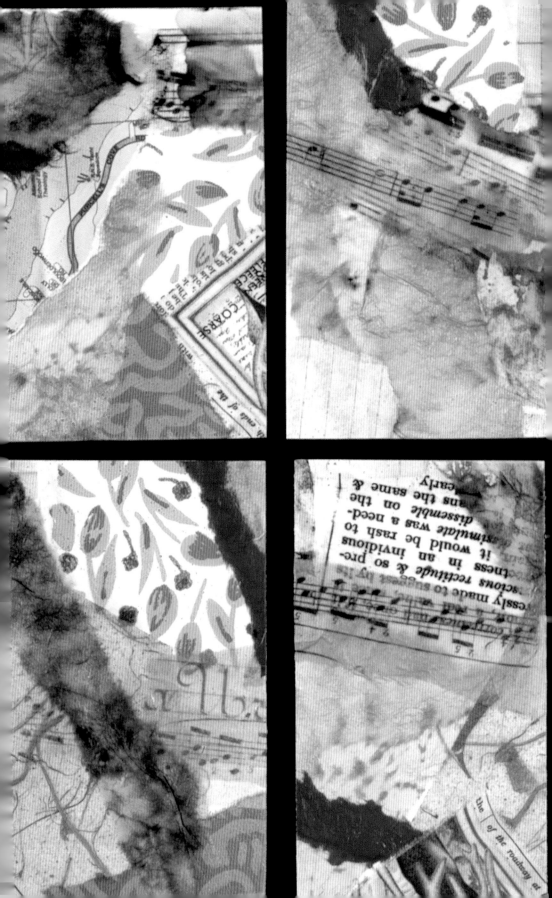

Project:
Collage Enlargement
Select small, appealing compositions within a collage.

Another exercise in painting with paper is one that I learned from Dawne Polis. She teaches high-school art and gives this project to her class as an introduction to mixed media.

1. Create an all-over random collage using any materials you choose. (See my all-over collage on page 23 for an example.)
2. Use a viewfinder to select small compositions within the collage that you find appealing, as I did in the small compositions shown.
3. Choose one of these small compositions and create an enlargement using collage, painting, and drawing (see my enlargement [above, left] of a small composition in the lower left image on page 62). Feel free to add texture and embellishment to enhance the composition. As a variation on this approach, try enlarging one of your artist trading cards (ATCs) in the same manner.

Put your blotting papers to work
I often use my used blotting papers as collage materials. I consider them a bonus, since they take no extra time or effort to create.

PLAYING WITH PAINT
Try incorporating painting and drawing in your collages.

There are several approaches to collage that involve painting and drawing:

- You can begin a collage by painting a background,
- Integrate painting and drawing into the collage process by painting between layers of collage elements, or
- Create your own painted collage materials.

Several paint application techniques can add interesting textures, colors, and depth to your collages. I covered large sheets of paper (24˝ x 18˝) with paint and gesso, using painting techniques as well as collage within the same piece. I call these my "paint playgrounds"—fun places to play and experiment with paint. They are never to be considered paintings in themselves, so I am not concerned about composition. I tear up the paint playgrounds for collage material or make them into book pages (see the double-page spreads on pages 140–141 that will be painted and collaged over). I used acrylic paints, glazes, and gesso for my paint playgrounds, but you could just as easily use watercolors or a combination of painting and drawing materials.

Each of the next three pages displays a large "paint playground" created as I've just described. Extracts from the large "playgrounds" are shown in the smaller illustrations, with text that describes the techniques I used.

Remember, you can always obscure parts of your paint playground and rework them with new colors and techniques.

When playing with paint, put a protective sheet of paper under the paper you are working on. This protective sheet, or blotting paper, acquires an interesting pattern of paint, and I often use mine as collage material.

Jane Davies: Paint playground 1, 24˝ x 18˝
Paint playgrounds allow you the freedom to paint with abandon, experimenting with any number of techniques and colors within the same piece.

Stamps are fun tools for creating repeated shapes and images
Use a sponge to apply acrylic paint to a stamp before stamping the paper. For the section shown here, I used a spiral stamp to create repeated shapes over the painted and gessoed surface.

Spatter paint with a stiff toothbrush
Make sure the paint is runny enough by diluting it with a bit of water, if necessary. Spattered paint adds texture and movement to the paint playground.

Apply acrylic glaze with a sponge
Let it dry slightly, and then spritz it with water. Let the water soak in for a minute or two, and then blot with a paper towel. This technique is most effective if the glaze is applied over another color. The spritz-and-blot technique leaves the impression of water droplets on your painting.

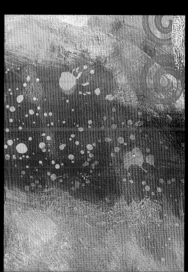

Fling paint or gesso onto your paper with a palette knife

Dip the palette knife into fluid paint, and hurl it onto the paper as if you are using your wand to cast a spell. Flung paint can add line and movement to your piece.

Jane Davies: Paint playground 2, 24˝ x 18˝
Add some lightweight collage elements to your paint playgrounds. In the section shown, in addition to the painting techniques, I added tissue paper, decorative paper, unryu, a paper doily, and some scraps of text printed out on lightweight paper.

Use a sponge to apply paint over a stencil

In the three images at the right, I used a vinyl scallop-shell stencil and a stencil made of perforated plastic ribbon (also known as sequin waste). In the top image, I used perforated ribbon as a stencil, carefully allowing the edges to fade into the background. I placed a paper doily on the section shown in the middle image and applied gesso with a sponge, which made a distinct lacy pattern. In the bottom section, I sponged paint through only part of the scallop-shell stencil to give more of a sense of depth and excavation rather than a clearly defined image.

Jane Davies: Paint playground 3, 24˝ x 18˝
Layering acrylic glazes and gesso in various techniques will always produce interesting collage material.

(top) Gesso texture under painting
Apply gesso or diluted gesso by brushing, spattering, using a palette knife, or employing any other techniques you choose. Leave some of the paper unpainted. Let the gesso dry completely, then sponge or brush on one or several colors of acrylic glaze (acrylic paint mixed with matte medium or glazing medium). The paint will be more intense in the places that are not gessoed, as the paper absorbs more of the paint than the gessoed areas. You can further enhance this difference by wiping some of the areas with damp paper towel, removing still more of the paint from the gessoed areas. You can see the pattern of gesso beneath the translucent applications of acrylic paint.

(above) Apply paint with a palette knife
Drag the palette knife over the surface lightly, leaving a thick, uneven application of paint. Here I used the dragging technique to apply two values of turquoise paint over the highly contrasting background.

WORKING IN LAYERS

Autumn Hathaway: The Big Apple (ATC)
Autumn enhanced her theme in every layer of this artist trading card (ATC).

Jane Davies: Angel Tally, 10˝ x 11˝
I began this piece with a random collage background, using wallpaper, maps, gesso textures, and handwriting.

Working in layers helps you see how materials and images relate to your theme.

We have considered collage in terms of gluing elements down to a support, and in terms of painting and piecing images in paper. In these discussions we have already made much use of the layering process. Here we will address more complex ways of layering, though first I want to discuss the creative dialogue you engage in with your materials and images as you work through a collage. Working in layers gives you a way to think about how the materials and images relate to your theme.

CREATIVE DIALOGUE

Observe the developing relationship of your materials, your ideas, and your collage. Often the path from blank support to finished collage takes many twists and turns.

The materials and techniques you choose for a collage are intricately intertwined with the ideas you express with them. You engage in a dialogue between form (materials and techniques) and content (ideas and themes), but they do not remain distinct entities. Some decisions in the process are made on formal grounds (I need a bright color here to balance out the darkness; I just like the way this shape looks next to this other shape), and sometimes on conceptual grounds (this piece is about my mother, so I would like to include some samples of her handwriting).

You may have an idea for a theme before you begin a collage. In this case, experiment with materials and process, finding your way intuitively to express the idea—finding your journey from raw materials to expressive piece. This is rarely a linear process. The materials you choose affect the original idea. As a theme evolves, your choice of materials and techniques may change accordingly. You may start with materials and images that inspire you and let ideas emerge from the process, building your image intuitively until it begins to speak to you, to suggest a theme. Many artists work in both ways, often within the same piece.

A theme for your collage may emerge at any point in the process. Sometimes a theme won't emerge until the collage is finished and you title it. The title then becomes the theme. More often than not, the theme will change or at lease shift during the process of making the collage.

The dialogue with your materials, your ideas, and the piece as it develops is the essence of the creative process. The more you engage in this process, the more attuned you become to the expressive qualities of materials and techniques. Working in layers is a way to observe this dialogue as it unfolds.

I will first outline a sequence of layers and then discuss other ways of layering. This sequence should in no way be considered a blueprint for layering, or directions for the right way to work in layers. It is merely one fairly simple and straightforward look at some different parts of a collage.

Autumn Hathaway's ATC "The Big Apple" (page 69) is a perfect example of straightforward layering—carrying a theme from the background through the final accents. She established the theme in the background by using a New York City map. She chose an apple as the central image. Then she toned down the background and emphasized the central image with paint. The words

"The Big Apple" add interest to the composition as well as give it a title. She included tiny round letters for a three-dimensional accent.

A collage docs not always happen in this straightforward a manner—background, image, more layering or additional elements, embellishment, title. Often the path from blank support to finished collage takes many twists and turns, steps backward, leaps forward, side trips, and stumbling over difficult places. And that journey is much of what makes it fun!

There are many ways of layering materials to build a collage. In the following discussion we will look at layering in terms of building from the background up, without obscuring or tearing away parts once they have

Autumn Hathaway: Journal page with watercolor background
Autumn often starts a new journal page by drawing with one or several watercolor crayons and then blending them with water.

been put in place. However, if the process takes you in a different direction, by all means take the new path.

BACKGROUNDS
Creating a background can jump-start the creative process.

Laying down a background on a blank piece of paper or canvas is a natural way to begin your creative journey into a collage. Whether you start with a theme in mind or a group of materials that inspire you, creating a background can jump-start the creative process. Sometimes when I am feeling stuck for ideas, I simply begin making backgrounds for future collages, and before I know it I am on a roll. The freedom of creating backgrounds instead of collages often loosens up whatever blockage is inhibiting my creative flow. I don't always use all of these backgrounds, but the ones that I don't use get recycled into collage materials one way or another.

Random Collage Backgrounds
Think of random collage backgrounds not as compositions, but as starting points.

The best materials to use for this kind of background are ones without explicit images. Go for colors, textures, text, maps, lists, etc., rather than pictures. Gather some collage materials and start cutting, tearing, and gluing them to your chosen supports. Do not think of these as collage compositions, but rather as starting points. You can always collage or gesso over the parts that don't work for the collages that you build on top of these backgrounds. Keep working this way, intuitively and without judgment, until you have a series or random collages that look to you like backgrounds begging for images. I usually work on three or four collage backgrounds at a time, using the same stash of materials.

If you have any trouble working with this kind of abandon, start with a small format. Create a series of ATC backgrounds, make backgrounds for your collage-a-day project, or make random collage backgrounds in your collage journal (see chapter 7).

Jane Davies: Hand Shake? 11″ x 9″
I used acrylic medium to transfer these images of women onto a random collage background. After many layers of paint, gesso, oil pastel, and more collage, the original background is barely visible. The mosaic-like collage on the right reminded me of Gustav Klimt's *The Kiss*, thus the title.

Jane Davies: Praying for Lemons, 12″ x 9″
This piece began as a somewhat geometrical collage of random materials, including recycled and digitally altered collages, decorative papers, my own handwriting, and translucent rice papers.

Random collage backgrounds

I used found text, maps, and my own artwork—much of it scanned and digitally altered—for these random collage backgrounds.

Structured Collage Backgrounds

The structured collage background is more deliberate than the random one. When you work with a structured collage background, you set up the main composition for the collage. For example, you may lay out your composition as a grid, a series of columns, or a landscape format. Your composition may change at any time during the collage process, but you set an intention at the beginning as you create the background.

Alix Hegeler: Untitled panel, 84″ x 28″
Alix begins her large-scale collages by layering dress patterns over newspaper printing plates. These provide the structure and geometry for her subsequent applications of collage, drawing, and painting.

Jane Davies: Handmade in Nepal, 8″ x 6″
An abstract landscape—uneven horizontal bands—is another type of structure for a collage background.

Unifying a Background with Gesso or Glaze

You may either proceed with your collage on the background as is, or tone down the contrasts somewhat by unifying the background with gesso or acrylic glaze. To do this, dilute some acrylic paint or gesso with matte medium or glazing medium and apply it over the whole surface of the collage background. While the surface is still wet, wipe it with a paper towel. If you want more color or more gesso, let it dry, and then apply another coat and wipe it again. You could simply apply one coat of glaze or diluted gesso to the collage background and let it dry. However, I find that applying it in successive layers and wiping each one gives you more control over the buildup of color or gesso, and allows you to obscure or reveal select parts of the collage underneath.

Gold-brown background

I made this random collage background with high-contrast papers, mostly black-and-white scribble drawings, and a striped decorative paper. I used a glaze of quinacradone gold acrylic paint to tone down the contrast and to give it a more unified look.

Jane Davies: Collage background unified with gesso

I applied a coat of diluted gesso to this collage background. This treatment virtually eliminates the contrasts, leaving more subtle variations in tone.

Painted and Textured Backgrounds

Sometimes a simple wash of watercolor or acrylic is enough to rid the support of its "blank canvas" characteristic. This may be all that you require to get started on a collage.

You can create a simple background with more intense color and depth by painting a textured support (canvas, or canvas with textured gesso application) with acrylic glaze (acrylic paint mixed with matte medium or glazing medium). Paint the whole surface with one coat of glaze, using one or several colors; wipe some of it off with a paper towel and let it dry. Build up a few layers of color this way until you have the effect you want. Sponge on a more concentrated glaze or some straight paint (paint with no added medium) around the edges, and blend with a paper towel.

Jane Davies: Acrylic glaze over gesso texture on canvas board
I applied gesso with a palette knife to canvas board, then scratched lines into it with a knitting needle. The canvas itself provides texture as well.

Jane Davies: Acrylic glaze over stretched canvas and canvas board
Examples of acrylic glaze applied to stretched canvas.

Autumn Hathaway: Journal page with stamped background
The result of wetting the page and stamping it with ink.

Unfinished Collage as a Background

Use an unfinished collage as a background or starting point for another.

If you have abandoned a collage or other piece of artwork in mid-stream, resurrect it by using it as a background or starting point for another collage. You may need to gesso or glaze over parts of it, or even collage a background over it. You can even cut it into pieces and rearrange them. Another way to approach this it to scan a finished or unfinished collage, or other artwork, and print out several copies on heavy photo paper. Then try several different ways of using it as a background.

Printed Material as a Background

Sometimes you can find ready-made backgrounds in the materials themselves. Using a piece of printed matter, such as a book page, sets the tone and structure of a collage, and it can also help to establish a theme. (See Dawne Polis's "Dictionary Page" series on page 95).

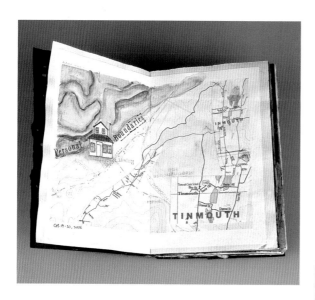

Jane Davies: Journal double-page spread "Personal Boundaries"
I chose this journal page, "Personal Boundaries," as a background for a new collage because its composition is relatively spare. I wanted to see how it would look with other elements layered over it. I scanned it and printed it out at its original size.

Jane Davies: "Personal Boundaries" used as a collage background, 11¹⁄₂″ x 6¹⁄₂″
I chose to cut the printout into sections and give the collage a vertical rather than a horizontal orientation.

IMAGE: THE NEXT LAYER
Try images on different backgrounds.

After the background is created, consider your central image. You can choose an image from your collection of materials (see "Praying for Lemons," on page 72, for my use of found imagery) or create one from bits and pieces, as Rowena Macleod did in "Flying to Paris" and "Paris." Try different images to see which one works best on your background. I find it liberating to work on several collages at once for this process, gathering background materials and images before beginning. Try different images on different backgrounds, and make changes where necessary.

(above) Rowena Macleod: Flying to Paris, 22˝ x 18˝
(opposite, top) Rowena Macleod: Paris, 12˝ x 8˝
In these two pieces, Rowena creates the figures from many diverse elements.

Ways of Applying an Image

You can glue down a ready-made image directly or use the gel transfer technique (see "Transferring an Image Using Acrylic Medium," on page 81, for how to create a translucent reverse version). I glued down the images in "Praying for Lemons" (page 72) directly. I transferred them in "Hand Shake?" (page 72).

Your image could be a cut-out shape made from paper in your collage stash or a silhouette cut from a solid-color paper, as in Autumn Hathaway's journal page showing a paper chain of little girls. In "Sunni-land" (page 80), Jane Maxwell makes effective use of the silhouette by repeating a shape in different materials. Another way to create a silhouette is to place a cut-out of your desired shape over the background and paint around it. This is known as masking technique. You could completely obscure the background around the image using several coats of gesso or paint ("Story Vessel") or use acrylic glaze and leave the background translucent (my journal page with Greek vases; both images on page 80).

Autumn Hathaway: Journal page
Autumn's blue paper chain of little girls reminds us, "Remember to play everyday." The bingo card provides a different context and another layer of meaning.

Jane Maxwell: Sunniland, 48˝ x 48˝
Jane uses the repeated silhouette to make a statement about our culture's insistence on uniformity in female body image.

Jane Davies: Journal page with Greek vases
One way to resolve a collage that is looking too complicated is to make it even more complicated, and then simplify and focus it using this masking technique. On this journal page I applied a transparent acrylic glaze around the masked shapes, leaving the layers of collage showing through in the background.

Jane Davies: Story Vessel, 7˝ x 5˝
In this collage I masked out a vase shape and then completely obscured the background with gesso. Then I added collage elements and applied an acrylic glaze of pthalo turquoise.

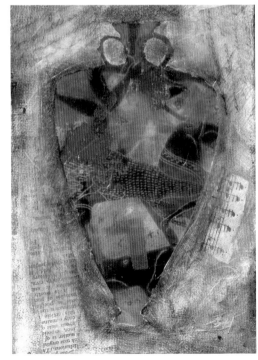

TRANSFERRING AN IMAGE USING ACRYLIC MEDIUM

Using this method to transfer an image to your collage, rather than gluing it directly, results in a more integrated look. Since the gel is translucent, you can see what is behind the image as well as the image itself. Remember that transferring will result in a reverse of the original. So, if it is important to have the original orientation, reverse the image using your photo-editing software before printing it out for a gel transfer.

Final image

This is how the image appears after it has been transferred. You can clearly see the graphics and text underneath it.

1. First, scan your image and print it out using an ink-jet printer. (See "Digital Alterations," on page 46, for tips on scanning and printing, and for ways of digitally altering your image before printing it.)

2. Choose the place on your background where you want the image to be. Cover the area with acrylic matte gel (gloss gel will work, too, but I prefer the finish that matte gel provides). Place the image face down on the gel, and press it firmly.

3. Leave it to dry thoroughly for several hours or overnight.

4. Wet the back of the paper with water, using a sponge or soft brush. Let the water soak in for a few minutes and then begin to peel the paper away. When the paper is peeled away, there will be some residual paper fiber still stuck to the gel in which the image has been preserved. Wet this and rub it with your finger (or even a scrub brush) repeatedly until there is no more white paper fiber left. If you have let the gel dry thoroughly, this scrubbing should not disturb the image. See "Final image," at left, for the successfully transferred image.

After I've soaked the paper, it is fairly easy to peel it away from the dried acrylic gel.

Be sure to rub away all the residual paper to get a clean transfer.

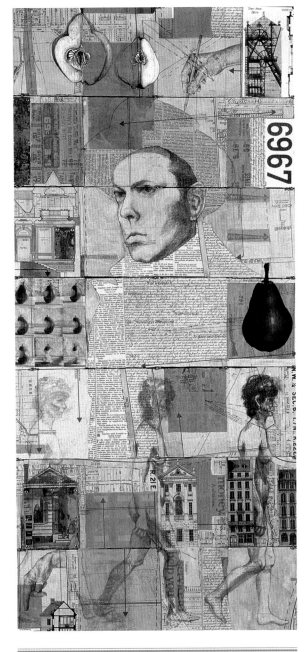

PAINTING AND DRAWING

It can be natural to combine collage with your own painted or drawn images.

Painting and drawing can be a way of creating the central image(s) of your collage. If you are a skilled painter or draftsperson and feel comfortable in this medium, it is a natural choice to combine collage with painted or drawn images of your own creation.

You can also use painting and drawing to enhance or alter a found image. You can augment the image by extending its lines or shapes or obscure part of it with painting or drawing. In my journal page "Personal Boundaries" (page 77), I extended some lines on the maps by drawing with permanent marker. I often apply paint in a light wash around an image to create a shadow-like effect, lifting it off the background.

Alix Hegeler: Untitled panel, 84˝ x 28˝
Alix hand-paints the pears and figures right over the collaged materials as her pieces develop.

Sharon McCartney: Bright Star Still Linger, 12˝ x 9˝
Sharon sometimes hand-paints and draws her birds and insects directly onto the collage, as in this piece, or applies them as photocopy transfers, as in "I Am Greatly Surprised" (see page 70).

FINISHING TOUCHES

Embellishments

Many collage artists use three-dimensional objects in their work—beads, buttons, ribbons, rhinestones, shells, game pieces, coins, jewelry parts, etc. They can be glued, sewn, wired, or attached by any other means you can think of.

Title

Finally, when you have finished a collage, give it a title. A title gives your piece a frame of reference that can inform its meaning. It also helps you to identify some of the possibly subconscious personal associations you make with your imagery and materials. Titling a piece challenges you to make these associations more conscious. If you are unsure about titling a piece, leave it untitled and come back to it later to see if something occurs to you.

Using the discussion above as a way to articulate the parts of a collage—background, image, painting and drawing, embellishment, and title—you can play with the order of the outlined sequence. For example, you may start with a found image, and then paint or collage a background around it rather than establishing the background first.

LAYERING COLLAGE WITH PAINT AND GESSO

Think about background and image as integrated parts of the whole.

Another way of building a collage is with successive layers of paper and gesso or paint. In this process you are thinking about background and image not necessarily separately, but as integrated parts of the whole. This method is great for exploring materials, colors, and compositions when you don't have a clear direction in mind. Whether an image or a theme develops or not, this process is an approach that emphasizes spontaneity.

Jane Davies: ATC
I used an artificial fingernail and some wired ribbon to bring this tiny collage to life.

Jane Davies: House Dream/Dream House, 12˝ x 10˝
After several layers of tissue paper, gesso, paint, and papers from my blue color stash, I added the house image and my own handwriting in pencil to give the piece focus and balance.

Jane Davies: High Tide, 12˝ x 10˝
I established the basic composition with layers of tissue paper, gesso, and paint. I emphasized the uneven quadrants by adding elements of decorative papers, magazine papers, and joss paper.

Project:
Tissue Paper and Paint Layering

Try an open-ended exploration rather than targeting a particular result.

In this project we start with tissue paper to create a basic composition, and then layer it with gesso, paint, and other papers. This is an open-ended exploration rather than a project with a particular result as a goal.

1. Choose several colors of tissue paper. Tear and cut it into a variety of shapes and sizes, then arrange the pieces on your support until you have a composition you like. Be spontaneous—don't agonize over your choices. You could work on three or four at once using the same colors so that you can try out different arrangements.

2. Glue the tissue to the support using matte medium: Brush the support with matte medium, and one at a time lay the pieces of tissue paper down, brushing the top with more medium. Let some of the pieces overlap, as in the photo of stage 1.

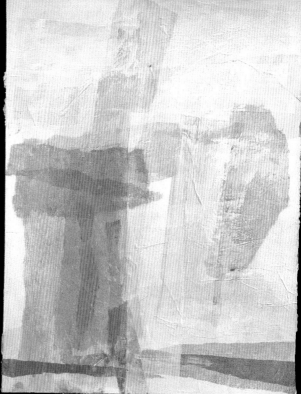

Layering tissue paper and paint, stage 1, 12″ x 10″
This is the first stage of my tissue-paper and paint collage.

Layering tissue paper and paint, stage 2, 12″ x 10″
I added more tissue paper, translucent white papers,
and gesso to the original composition. This piece eventually
evolved into "After the Explosion" (page 117).

3. Let the matte medium dry to the touch. Then apply gesso and/or watered-down gesso to some parts of the collage.

4. When the gesso is dry, apply more colored tissue paper, translucent white papers, or textured papers such as unryu or lace papers, if you like, and more gesso as needed. See the photo of stage 2.

5. Keep building your collage in this manner until you have an arrangement that you like. You may hit a winning composition right away, or it may take several layers. Remember you can always use gesso to "ghost back" or completely obscure previous layers of tissue paper. "Veiling" with gesso and then adding fresh bright tissue papers or glazes selectively gives your piece visual depth.

6. Now, choosing papers from your collage materials and/or color stashes, add a few elements to the tissue-paper collage. You may continue to develop an abstract composition, or introduce an image at this point.

7. Once these papers are glued down to your liking, you may consider your collage complete, or continue adding and layering until it feels complete.

Jane Davies: My Sister and I Were Close Like That, 5˝ x 4˝
Jane Davies: House Floating, 6˝ x 4˝
Jane Davies: Collage study, 6˝ x 4˝
I created this group of small collage studies using the technique described for "High Tide" (page 84), except that I added a coat of acrylic gloss medium between some of the layers of paint and collage, providing the final piece with a greater sense of depth.

LAYERING WITH GEL MEDIUM

Bring depth and clarity to a collage by using layers of acrylic gloss medium or gel.

You can create a sense of depth and clarity by applying collage materials and paint between layers of acrylic gloss medium or gel. I recommend gloss rather than matte medium or gel because it remains perfectly transparent even through many layers.

LAYERING WITH TRANSPARENT MATERIALS

Experiment by layering imagery on transparent and translucent materials.

A variety of transparent materials

You can create transparent or translucent collage materials by printing on vellum, printable organza, printable transparent plastic, or lightweight papers from your computer.

Transparent materials give you the ability to layer images and patterns over one another without completely obscuring previous layers. The design beneath will be more or less visible depending on the particular qualities and degree of transparency of the material covering it. Vellum, for example, has a diffuse translucent quality that renders an image beneath it soft and ghostly. Organza, on the other hand, is much more transparent. Because of its loose weave, an image printed on organza appears more apparition-like than the pattern or image behind it.

Transparent plastic, such as Graphix, gives you the ability to create images that are perfectly transparent (except where the ink is), like the layers of an anatomy diagram. Lightweight papers, such as unryu, lightweight

mulberry paper, and onion skin, have their own unique qualities. Experiment by printing, transferring, painting, or drawing imagery on transparent and translucent materials, and layering them in collage.

I printed images from my computer onto translucent tissue-weight paper (sumi paper, just stiff enough to go through the printer), organza (Extrav-Organza—a printer-friendly organza backed with paper that peels off after printing), and vellum, and used these materials to create "House Dream" and "Walk in the Woods" (page 88). In "To the Evening Star" and "Sincerity" (page 36), Sharon McCartney layers delicate antique white linens over printed materials. The translucence of the linens lets the viewer see the imagery underneath.

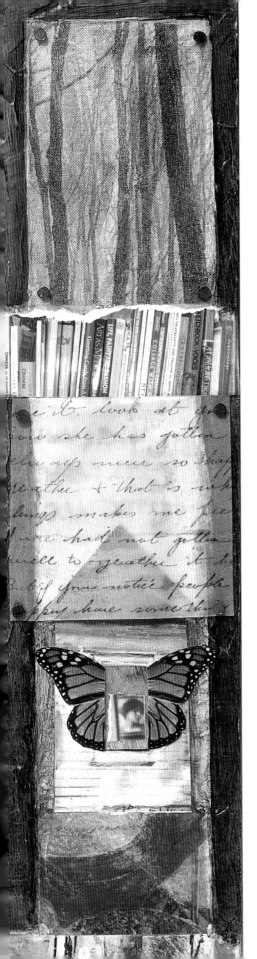

Jane Davies: House Dream, 11˝ x 3˝, on wood
The organza (top) and vellum (center) are attached to the wood support with small tacks so that these transparent materials float just above the image beneath.

Jane Davies: Walk in the Woods, 8 ¹/₂˝ x 6˝
I used layers of translucent printed papers, printed organza, and paper silhouettes to create the rhythm of a repeated image. The forest imagery is digitally altered from my own photographs and printed on sumi paper and organza.

Making Gel Transparencies

In addition to tissue-weight papers, translucent fabrics, and other materials, you can create gel transparencies by using acrylic gloss medium and ink-jet prints.

1. Scan and print an image on your ink-jet printer.
2. Brush it with a coat of acrylic gloss medium or gel. Let it dry completely and apply another coat. Repeat until you have about four coats of medium on your image. Let the whole thing dry overnight.
3. Cut out the image close to its edges, leaving a little bit of overhang. Soak it in water for a few minutes.
4. Peel the paper away from the gel.
5. Place the gel transparency face down on your worktable. Wet the back, and rub away the paper residue with your finger. For a faster technique, use a scrub brush, but be careful not to damage the gel transparency.

This process is very much like doing an acrylic gel transfer (see "Transferring an Image Using Acrylic Medium," on page 81), but instead of transferring the image onto another image, you are transferring the image only to the gel. Later you can apply it to a collage in progress.

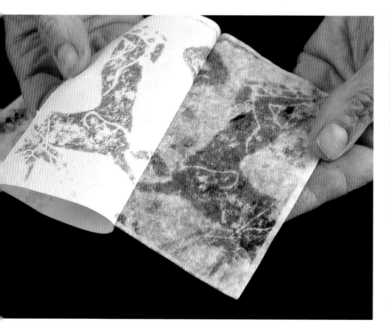

Peeling paper away from gel on a gel transparency
Wetting the paper and letting it soak for a few minutes makes it pliable enough that you can peel it away from the gel.

Rubbing the paper residue off the gel transparency
Peeling the paper away removes the bulk of it from the gel transparency, but a little elbow grease is required to get the rest of it off.

Group of gel transparencies
Gel transparencies tend to curl and wrinkle a bit until you apply them to a collage surface. Once adhered, they lie flat.

Jane Davies: Collage study made with one of the gel transparencies, 10˝ x 12˝
Gel transparencies add depth and complexity to this otherwise simple collage.

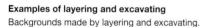

Examples of layering and excavating
Backgrounds made by layering and excavating.

LAYERING AND EXCAVATING
Create a complex background by adding and subtracting until the piece is done.

This is a process of layering collage materials with paint, glazes, and gesso, and then tearing parts of the materials away, adding and subtracting until you are satisfied with the piece. This can be a way to create a complex background in the layering process described above, or a way to build an image into a finished collage.

Here is how to make a layered and excavated background:

1. Cover your support with acrylic matte medium and apply strips of collage papers. In one example (above, left) I used torn book pages and other found text.

2. Brush matte medium or acrylic glaze over the collaged papers. Add another layer of collage papers and matte medium or glaze. Let it dry to the touch.

3. Apply a coat of gesso and let it dry to the touch.

4. Peel away some of the collaged papers. They are likely to tear and make interesting shapes, rather than peel away cleanly. If they are coming off the support without tearing, let the piece dry a little longer.

5. Repeat steps 3 and 4, if you like. Then apply another coat of gesso. Let it dry for several hours or overnight.

6. Sand the top layer of gesso to varying degrees in different areas of the collage. You can control the effect by varying the grade of sandpaper and how much you sand it.

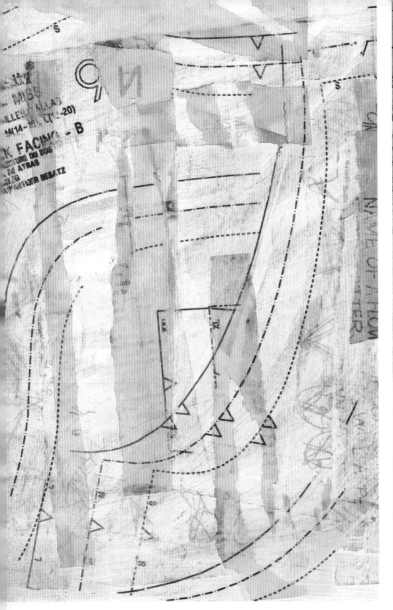

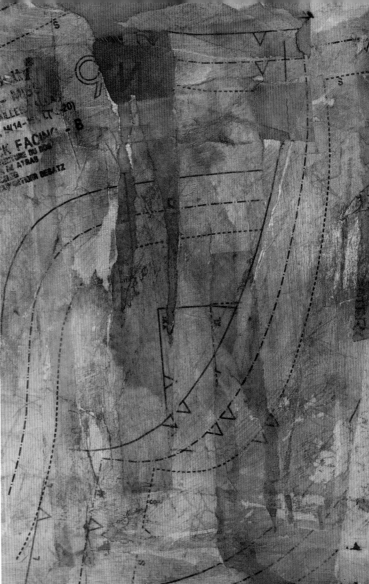

You can continue building up layers in this manner, applying collage papers, matte medium, acrylic glaze, and gesso, and then peeling off the papers and sanding through the gesso, until you are satisfied with the result. Now you can use it as a background, or modify it by adding layers of acrylic glaze, as I did in the examples on this page.

In the background shown at the left on page 91 I used a quinacradone gold acrylic glaze to build up the layers. In the one at the right on page 91 I used a red-and-orange scribble drawing as the support.

Example of layering and excavating
An example of layering and excavating with various papers and gesso.

Layering and excavating with an acrylic glaze
The same background with the addition of acrylic glazes and iridescent pigments.

Creating a series lets you explore possible solutions and avenues for arriving at them. Be open to the unexpected.

Working in series means working on a group of collages, either all at once, or sequentially, that are based on one theme. The theme can be broad, encompassing a number of sub-themes, or very specific. It could also be a group of ideas you want to weave together over the course of a series of collages.

One can view art as a kind of aesthetic problem-solving in which there is never only one solution. Working in series allows you the freedom to explore many possible solutions and a variety of avenues for arriving at those solutions. An aesthetic problem can be as simple as "How can I put these particular materials together in this particular format, and make it work?" It can also be something more conceptual, such as "How can I visually express the idea of precarious balance?" Imagery can also be the glue that holds a series together, the aesthetic question being "How many ways can I use this particular type of imagery?" or "Why am I so fascinated by this imagery? What does it mean to me?"

Many artists tackle a number of interwoven aesthetic and conceptual issues within one series. They set up a number of different parameters that either define, or become the springboard for, a series.

Alix Hegeler based her series of large-format panel collages on a group of materials that fascinated her: newspaper printing plates, British tabloids, dress patterns, etc. To these she added her own paintings and drawings of figures, pears, and other images, weaving together a rich tapestry of ideas within her chosen format. This series has been in progress for several years and is an ongoing process. (See, for example, her untitled panel on page 82.)

Erika Schmidt based her "Unfolding" series on the image of a

Sharon McCartney: Only This, 12˝ x 9˝
Sharon McCartney works on groups of pieces all at once, and they sometimes result in series.

fan, but within that there are many themes and sub-themes. "Unfolding" serves as an umbrella theme, within which she explores various kinds of materials and imagery. (See her collages on page 61.)

IDEAS FOR SERIES

I suggest that you do many of the projects and exercises in this book in series, including "One Object, Ten Collages" and ATCs from chapter 1; the "Collage-a-Day" exercise from chapter 2; "Tissue-Paper Collage" and "Cut-Paper Collage" from chapter 3; "Tissue Paper and Paint Layering" from chapter 4; and "Playing with Context" and "Personal Iconography" from chapter 6. Any of the other projects and suggestions could be the basis of a series as well. To explore more ideas for series, try any of the following:

- Assemble a group of materials that you find interesting or challenging. Create a series of collages using primarily those materials. See how the materials themselves can express a range of moods or ideas. Be open to the unexpected. Themes may emerge that you had not intended or thought of.

- Choose an idea from your idea list (see chapter 2) and use the series format to explore ways to express that idea visually.

- Gather a type of imagery that either has special meaning for you or that holds metaphorical possibility (see chapter 6 for a discussion of symbolic and metaphorical imagery). Make a series of collages using that imagery to express the themes it suggests to you.

Sharon McCartney: Solitude, 12″ x 9″
Sharon McCartney: Joining In, 12″ x 8″
Sharon's "Bird Languages" series, for example, are tied together by theme, materials, layout, and imagery.

(opposite) **Dawne Polis: Dictionary Page series, 9″ x 6″**
Dawne is fascinated by old dictionaries that are heavily illustrated. She used some particularly choice pages from such a book as the basis for this series. Dawne created all of the collages in this series in one sitting, exploring the theme of meaning in language, pictures, diagrams, and symbols.

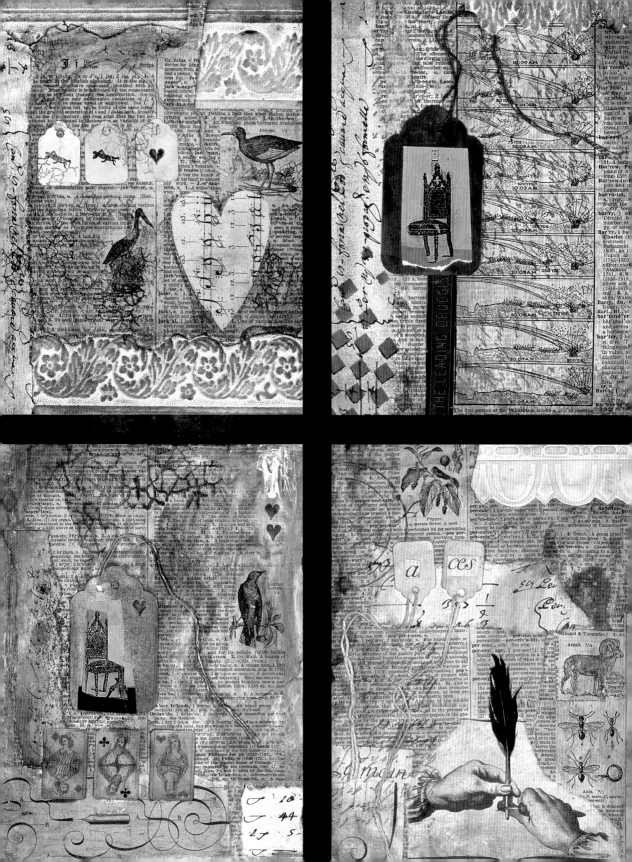

USING TEXT IN COLLAGE

Incorporating text can add a layer of meaning or an evocative visual element.

Text is a powerful tool to use in collage, a medium that is primarily visual. If a collage seems not quite focused or resolved, sometimes adding text can nail it. In using words in your collage, it is not only *what* is written, but how the writing *looks* on the page. Incorporating text can add another layer of meaning or an evocative visual element, create a pattern or texture, or suggest communication or hidden meaning.

First, we will explore the many different sources of text available for collage and experiment with techniques for creating your own text. Then we will discuss the use of text as a visual element and as a conveyor of meaning.

FOUND TEXT
Use words and phrases for their content or their visual effect.

Using found text can result in unexpected meanings and juxtapositions with images. Newspapers, junk mail, prescriptions, magazines, your own written journal, discarded books, take-out menus, concert programs, receipts, tickets, brochures, business cards, flyers, packaging—all these and more are easily accessible sources of found text. I suggest keeping a stash of text separate from your other collage materials. Some of the text will be specific words and phrases that you may want to use for their content, and some will be primarily for visual effect. Once you start looking for and collecting text from different sources, you will appreciate the vast array of expressive potential that it offers.

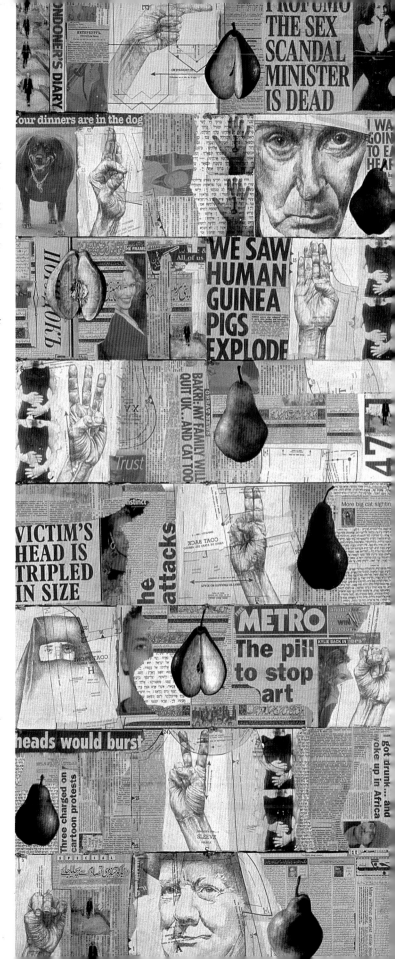

Alix Hegeler: Untitled panel, 84″ x 28″
Alix uses text both as a formal element (for texture, pattern, and its graphic quality), and as a conveyor of meaning. See detail at left.

CREATING TEXT

Creating your own text allows you the freedom to choose your words without searching them out from found sources. You can simply type out your desired text on your computer, put it in the font that best expresses your intended mood, size it appropriately, and print it on the paper of your choice. And there are many more ways to create your own text for use in collage.

- **Handwriting.** Try your own handwriting using different tools—ballpoint pen, fountain pen, pencil, marker, etc. See my example of handwriting with different tools.
- **Sgraffito handwriting in gesso with glaze.** Apply gesso to your support using a brush. While wet, use a knitting needle or other pointed tool to write into the gesso. Let dry completely, then apply a coat of acrylic paint mixed with matte medium or glazing medium. Wipe some of the paint off with a paper towel. ("Palm Reading," on page 101, is an example.) You can also sgraffito handwriting or other lettering directly into wet paint. See my example.
- **Stamped letters.** Try different types of letter stamps to create text, either using a stamp pad or sponging acrylic paint onto the stamps before pressing them onto the paper.
- **Cut-out letters.** Cut letters out of collage papers.
- **Crayon resist with watercolor or acrylic wash.** Use a white crayon or clear oil pastel to write on your paper. Dampen the paper with water, and then apply a coat of watercolor or acrylic wash. While the paper is wet, you can add more washes of paint or thinned gesso.
- **Stenciled letters.** Letter stencils are widely available in hardware stores as well as hobby and art-supply stores. I use a sponge to apply acrylic paint through the stencil, but you can try other application techniques. Letter stencils often have a bold graphic look. Use dif-

Jane Davies: Example of handwriting with different tools
I experimented with handwriting styles using metallic marker, gel pen, ballpoint, graphite stick, and white oil pastel over a painted journal page.

Jane Davies: Examples of writing with crayon resist
I used light-colored oil pastel on watercolor paper for the writing, then applied washes of acrylic paint and gesso, blotting them in places, to create the variegated background.

ferent stencils within the same word or phrase in order to try out the effect of a different style for the various letters.

- **Transfer letters.** Press-type or rub-ons are available in individual letters in many different fonts, and as words and phrases. You can find them in the scrapbooking or card-making section of your local craft or hobby store.

Dawne Polis: The Joy of the Play House, 10˝ x 8˝
Dawne used a children's book page as the inspiration for this nostalgic, playful collage about herself and her husband, Dean.

TEXT AS A VISUAL ELEMENT

Fragmented or obscured text or text in a foreign language can be mysterious.

Aside from its obvious role of conveying meaning verbally, text also has the power to evoke meaning visually. Consider the different associations we have with the following: a newspaper clipping, a handwritten letter or journal page, e-mail, a typed note, a stenciled sign, Chinese calligraphy, a magazine advertisement, a Latin manuscript, junk mail, directions for assembling your stereo, a handwritten recipe, etc. Each one of these can evoke a context or mood whether you can read the words or not. For example, in "Palm Reading" (page 101), the words suggest some kind of meaning or communication, but they are completely illegible.

There is something mysterious about fragmented or obscured text, or text in a foreign script or language. The viewer is not expected to read it literally, but it still holds the suggestion of a message, communication, meaning, without specifics. (See Alix Hegeler's untitled panel on page 97.)

TEXT AS A CONVEYOR OF MEANING

Text in a collage can inform the way an image is perceived.

Text can also convey meaning directly, as it does in many of the examples shown in this chapter and elsewhere. Many artists use text in two ways within the same piece. Alix Hegeler's large-scale collages contain foreign text, obscured and fragmented (that is, illegible) text, as well as bold tabloid headlines that scream out at the viewer. (Alix's untitled panels on pages 74, 82, and 97 are examples.) All use pieces of text to add visual texture and depth as well as verbal associations with the images.

Text in a visual format informs the way we perceive an image by imposing a specific context. Just for fun, and to demonstrate this principle, try the following exercise:

Word-Image Association

1. Cut out a dozen or more words and phrases from found text. Magazines and junk mail are good sources for this exercise.
2. Gather about the same number of ready-made images—from magazines, your personal snapshots, catalogs, newspapers, etc.
3. Randomly assign the words or phrases to the images, and see how each word-image association strikes you. Some are likely to resonate in some way, and some will not.
4. Rearrange the words and phrases so they are assigned to different images. Observe how you perceive the images with their new verbal associations.

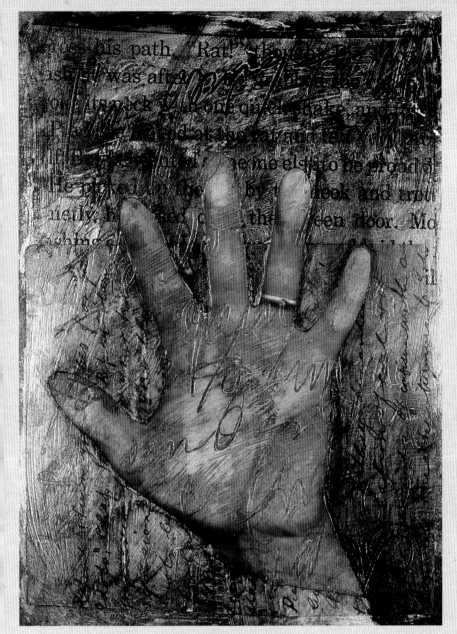

Jane Davies: Palm Reading, 8˝ x 6˝
The title of this piece brings attention to the text, though none of
it is legible. The text provides both visual and conceptual texture.

Project:
Using Text as
a Visual Element

1. Working in a small format, tear some
pieces of found text and collage them onto
your support.

2. Partially obscure the background by
one or several layers of acrylic glaze. Add
more collage and glaze until you are satisfied with the background.

3. Choose an image as the focal point of
your collage. Glue it in place and let dry.

4. Apply acrylic matte medium or gel to
the entire collage. While it is wet, sgraffito some handwriting into the gel. Let dry
completely.

5. With a sponge or brush, apply a dark
color of acrylic paint to the collage, making sure to get it into all the crevices of your handwriting.

6. Wipe the excess off with a paper towel. You can remove more of the glaze in some areas by dampening
the paper towel. Repeat the glazing and wiping until
you are satisfied with the result. This technique brings
up subtle textures in the surface.

7. At this point your collage may be finished, or you
may want to add to it, embellish it, or make it part of
a bigger piece. The choice is yours.

Cynthia Gregory: Mr. So and So, 3″ x 2″ each panel

Cynthia found all of the text for this piece in one issue of *The New Yorker* magazine. The piece came together in a single sitting after she had collected and played with the materials over a period of time.

Project:
Creating Narrative from Found Text

A story can emerge from unexpected associations.

Once you begin collecting and playing with found text and pairing it with different types of imagery, you gain an understanding of how a story can emerge from unexpected associations. For this project, use as much found text as possible. If you need to fill in a word here and there that you can't find, create it on your computer or with letter stickers or stamps. Relying mostly on found text, rather than text you create, sets the stage for unex-pected associations and meanings. You may, for example, find a piece of text that you feel compelled to use but that does not relate in an obvious way to your original idea. It may inspire a whole new narrative, or push your story in a surprising direction, bringing new meaning to your images. This project is about the process of discovering how narrative can emerge from words and images, rather than about telling and illustrating a story.

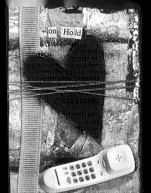    

Jane Davies: Falling Awake, 3 ½˝ x 2 ½˝ each panel
I made many small panels over a period of a few weeks,
arranging and rearranging pieces of text and images. The text
came from several sources.

There is no right way to start this project. You could be inspired by some found text, or you may have a story you want to tell. When you are playing with your scraps or looking at a group of ATCs you've just created, the images may inspire you to arrange them into a narrative and pair them with text. Your collage journal may be a source for an idea for this project (see chapter 7).

1. If you don't have a particular inspiration but want to try this project, then I suggest gathering materials and imagery and just start making a series of collages. I recommend using a small format so that you can work quickly and spontaneously. You might include imagery in some, and leave others as abstract compositions. (See "Working in Series," on page 93, for more about what constitutes a series.)

2. Go through your sources of text and cut out words and phrases that appeal to you. Don't edit, just cut. Build yourself a stash of words and phrases from as many sources as you can find. The ones you don't use in this project will find their way into, or perhaps even inspire, other projects.

3. Start pairing the found text with your collages. Make adjustments in your collages if the text inspires you to do so, adding imagery or glazes of color, or collaging over parts that no longer work. Or, create more collages to accommodate the text. This process is truly a dialogue between the visual collage and the text, so keep your mind open to unexpected juxtapositions.

4. Remember, this is not intended to be a plotted story line, so don't worry about the words describing the images or the images illustrating the text. Just keep pairing text with image, finding more text and creating more collage images as you feel you need to. Glue down the text fragments.

5. Look at your whole series of collages with text, and start putting them in order. Try different orders. You don't need to use all of them. Sometimes only a few in your series will hang together and make a stronger narrative than if you had used all of them.

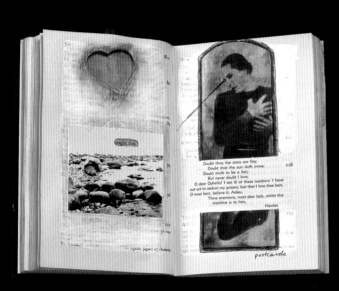

Sue Wright: LET HAM/HAMLET, altered book, 7˝ x 5˝
In Sue Wright's altered book, she created a story within
the story by choosing bits of text from each page. Her collages
and drawings both create and enhance the new story.

Dawne Polis: Mother, altered book, 7˝ x 5˝
For a book to her mother, Dawne used religious material from the
original book as well as a found letter.

How did you know where to find

home

?

you said

a little

the new house would feel

UNUSUAL

Jane Davies: Through the Looking-glass, 8 ½" x 7 ½"
My study in using selective found text.

Project:
Found-Text Collage

Tailor the text by obscuring some words with gesso, acrylic paint, or pastel.

Both Dawne Polis and Sue Wright have created altered book collages in which the text is chosen by obscuring all non-chosen words with gesso and acrylic paint or water-soluble oil pastel. I was inspired by these pieces to create this project. These directions are for doing this process as a freestanding collage rather than as a book.

1. Adhere one or several pieces of text to your collage support. If you choose several, you can orient the text in different directions if you like.

2. Choose some words and phrases from the text that you would like to feature in your collage. You can add words from other sources as well by gluing them down in the appropriate places. Don't forget to leave room for images and other collage elements.

3. Apply gesso, diluted gesso, or an acrylic glaze to the areas around your chosen words, either veiling or completely obscuring them.

4. Collage your image and other elements in place. Add a border or embellishments, or anything else you like, until your collage feels complete.

To do this project as an altered book, follow the instructions in chapter 7, but leave the words you've chosen exposed.

MEANING AND PERSONAL EXPRESSION

There is no such thing as the one correct interpretation of an image.

When we say a collage or an image is meaningful, what are we saying? Does an image have meaning beyond a subjective response? If my collage has one meaning for me, and a completely different meaning for you, have I failed as an artist to convey my message? If I have a specific intention as to a collage's meaning and you don't get it as a viewer, is the collage meaningless?

Meaning includes the whole impact that an image has on us—the representational or literal, the metaphorical connections, the symbolic, the subjective, the evocative nature of color and other formal elements, and everything in between. "A picture is worth a thousand words" gets at the fact that images speak in ways that words can't.

The viewer brings to an image his or her own sensibility and experience, thereby coloring his or her interpretation. To this extent the meaning of the piece is subjective: You and I may literally see the same thing when we look at an image, but usually we make different personal connections to it. I look at an image of seaweed and feel nostalgic for my Nova Scotia childhood. You may experience the same image as menacing if you associate seaweed with a traumatic boating accident. There is just no such thing as *the* one correct-singular-absolute interpretation of an image, but rather a whole host of meanings that are interpreted differently by different viewers.

This is not to say that viewing a work of art is a completely subjective and unique experience for each person.

Jane Davies: Detail from Sea-ing Green, 10″ x 10″
I often experiment with images of seaweed, as well as the rough and rusted surfaces found around fishing docks, to explore memories of my Nova Scotia childhood.

Beyond our subjective interpretations, there are many ways in which we share meanings of images to greater and lesser extents. For example, in Rowena McLeod's "Gun Kite" (page 108), we probably all agree that it is a picture of a boy in front of a fence flying a kite that is a gun. We probably further agree that there is something menacing or mysterious about the casual attitude of the boy and the fiery intensity of the sky. However, we may have different personal associations with guns, toys (the kite), or fences. The sky in this image could remind some people of fireworks, and others of destruction.

CONTEXT AND METAPHOR
Collage can put images and materials in new contexts.

The context of an image is an important part of its meaning. Webster's defines *context* as "the set of circumstances or facts surrounding a particular event, situation, etc." Just using an image or material in a collage is giving it new circumstances and surroundings. Collage is all about taking imagery and materials out of their original contexts, or circumstances, and putting them in new ones. At its best, collage is about recontextualizing materials, giving them new life and new meaning.

In "Flying to Paris" (page 78), Rowena McLeod uses a picture of a boat for part of a woman's dress, giving the boat an entirely different context and therefore new meaning. In Alix Hegeler's collages (for example, the detail of a panel showing some of her diverse materials on page 34), she uses dress patterns for their graphic geometric qualities. They are no longer to be understood as guidelines for cutting dress fabric, but as lines, words, arrows, and other graphic elements. The seaweed and the blue, wave-like shapes make the silhouette figure in my journal double-page spread "Over the Deep End/Coming Up for Air" (page 136), read as floating in water rather than the yoga relaxation posture it originally illustrated.

**Rowena Macleod: Gun Kite,
11″ x 9″**
Rowena worked with themes
of violence and childhood—the
idea that we want to protect our
children from the dangers of
the world.

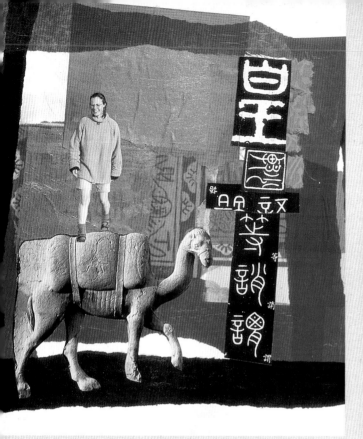

Project:
Playing with Context
Place an image on several different backgrounds.

Cut out or create an image of anything you choose. It can be a figure, a house, a vehicle, a book, a toothbrush, a flower—anything from any source. Scan and print multiple copies of it (or photocopy it). Now, create several backgrounds using any of the suggestions in chapter 4, or create settings such as a landscape, an interior space, a window, a house, a garden, an underwater scene, a doorway, an altar or shrine, etc. Alternatively, you could search through your collage recycling bin and use unfinished collages as the backgrounds. Place the images on the backgrounds, arranging and rearranging them, and noticing how the background informs the interpretation

Jane Davies: Camel Journey, 10″ x 9¹/₂″
Jane Davies and Amanda Smith: Path, 7¹/₂″ x 5¹/₂″
I used a photograph of myself to play with context, using old or unfinished collages as backgrounds

of the image. Add other images if that seems right, and see how they also affect the meaning of your primary image. If you like, take this process further by giving your pieces titles or adding text in some other way, as described in chapter 5.

METAPHOR

When you use visual metaphor, an object takes on new attributes.

In its simplest form, metaphor is a transfer of meaning from one object or situation to another. We usually think of this phenomenon in terms of language. It serves as a kind of shorthand by which many properties can be attributed to an object or situation with one word or phrase. Our everyday speech is rich with metaphor; for example, to say someone's opinion is a little off base, or that a person is out in left field is not to say that they are playing baseball. When my creative juices are flowing, I am not getting all wet; when my creative well runs dry I am not literally thirsty. So ubiquitous is the use of metaphor that we would be hard-pressed to speak without it. In fact, "hard-pressed" itself is a metaphor.

Visual metaphor works in the same was as linguistic metaphor. You put one thing in the context of another thing, making it into that other thing, metaphorically—transferring the attributes of the new context onto the object. In "Gun Kite" (page 108), for example, the gun is

Jane Davies: Putting Down Roots, 14″ x 11″
I used an altered photograph of my house, a scan of my hands, and a lot of textural collage and paint. Because the house looks as if it is about to be swept up into the stormy sky, an alternate title is "Holding On with All I've Got."

Jane Davies: Palm Trees, 7″ x 5″
A play on words. I scanned my hand, then altered the colors in Photoshop before using them in the collage.

made into a kite, and thus into a plaything, just by putting it on the end of a string that the boy is holding and adding a tail to it. The metaphor gives us pause, gives us food for thought. What does it mean to say a gun is like, or is being used like, a plaything? What is so disturbing about the image and about that thought? In my "Putting Down Roots" (above), the image of the house becomes a plant that is "rooted" by hands reaching down into the soil. The metaphor raises the question "What is it about my hands that keeps me 'rooted' or allows me to 'put down roots'?" "Palm Trees" (above) is more of a visual interpretation of a play on words, making the palms of my hands into the tropical treetops.

Jane Davies: Roof Over My Head, 10″ x 10″
I was thinking of how much my living (the metaphorical roof over my head) depends on a global economy, on a world outside my immediate community.

Project:
Simple Visual Metaphor

"Gun Kite" (page 108), "Palm Trees" (page 110), and "Putting Down Roots" (page 110) all make use of simple visual metaphors, in that they put one kind of object in the context of another, thus shifting its meaning. For this project, make a series of collages based on such visual metaphors. Here are some suggestions, though once you get started you will undoubtedly come up with your own ideas.

- Use various kinds of objects for the petals or blooms of a flower, or the limbs of a tree.
- Create your own version of "Putting Down Roots," substituting your own imagery for the house and the hands.
- In "Roof Over My Head," I use Chinese currency for the roof and postage stamps for the windows in a house image. Create a house collage using different imagery for windows, doors, and roof.
- Head, heart, and hands hold a lot of metaphorical weight. Create a collage figure or series of figures, playing with different imagery for the head, heart (or torso), and hands.

SYMBOL AND ICON
Symbolic images can have multiple meanings, from the universal to the personal.

A symbol is a mark or image that stands for something else, usually something specific. Symbolic marks—the letters of an alphabet, hieroglyphs, Chinese characters, peace signs, Celtic runes—derive their meanings from cultural convention. Such graphic symbols may have had their origins in pictorial representation but have evolved into abstract marks to such an extent that they need to be specifically learned in order to be understood.

A symbolic image, or icon, is similar in that its meaning is derived from its cultural context. The Virgin Mary, the *Mona Lisa*, the Golden Arches, and the Campbell's soup can, for example, are all rich with symbolic cultural associations. However, their meanings are open to interpretation. Depending on the viewer and the context, symbolic images can have meanings that range from the universal to the culturally specific to the personal. When we use found imagery in collage, we take advantage of its cultural and personal symbolic associations. By working with imagery repeatedly, and reflecting on our choices, we can develop a vocabulary of personal iconography— that is, images that have symbolic significance for us.

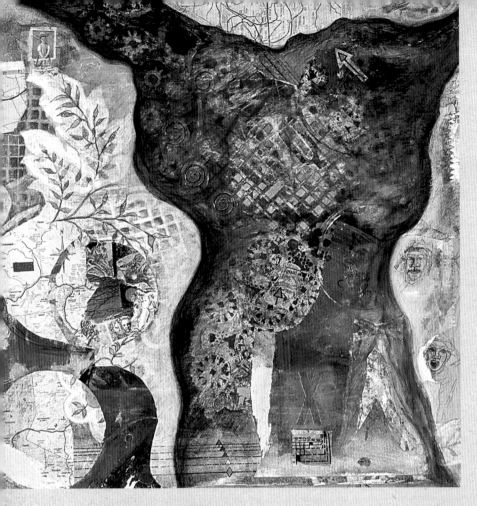

Cynthia Gregory: Motherland, 19″ x 19″
Rivers and maps are part of Cynthia's personal iconography, symbolizing "where I've been and where I'm going," both in time and in space.

Jane Davies: Examples of personal iconography project
I used images of my books, my truck, and a canning jar, among others, to explore my personal iconography.

Project:
Personal Iconography

Make a list and write down anything that comes into your head.

In this project we develop a group of images that speak to us personally. They may have no particular meaning to anyone else, but that does not matter.

1. Make a list of objects that represent you in some way. They can be things that symbolize your hobbies and interests, your personality, your profession, pet peeves, anything that says something about you. Don't think too hard about this—just make a list and write down anything that comes into your head. If you are a musician or music enthusiast, it might be sheet music or a particular instrument or a CD; if you are a gardener, it could be your favorite plant or vegetable or a garden tool. If you paint, it could be tubes of paint, brushes, etc. My list includes the canning jar that appears in two of the images at the right, various cooking utensils, a wine bottle, a garden spade, a cat, books, art supplies, my wood stove, my pickup truck, and many other things representing my domestic, artistic, rural life. Once you have your list, find images of as many of the objects as you can, or take photographs of them. (I took photos of my truck, my teapot, my bookshelves, and other things.)

2. Photocopy or scan and resize them to a scale that will work with your chosen format.

3. Choose some collage materials for your backgrounds and create a series of backgrounds on a group of small supports. I used watercolor paper cut to 5″ x 3½″ with simple painted backgrounds, as well as discarded collages cut to the same size.

4. Start playing with your images, putting them together in different ways. See how they speak to you in different contexts.

Sharon McCartney: All I Could Think, book format
Sharon McCartney: For Thoughts of Past and Future, book format
Sharon uses the book format to encourage the viewer to see her work intimately, taking the time to "read" it as you would a book. The book format suggests a narrative or journal, and thus influences the way you interact with it.

FORMAT

What kind of object is your collage?

By format, I mean what kind of object your collage is. Is it flat art that is to be viewed as "art on the wall"? Is it the size of a sheet of plywood such that it must be viewed from a distance, or is it on a scale that demands a more intimate look? Is it a singular, self-contained piece, or is it part of a series meant to be viewed as a group? Is it a page in your private collage journal? Your collage might be in the form of a codex (a book bound at the spine) that must be read one double-page spread at a time, or an accordion book that stands up on its own. Joshua Porter created a series of collages as prayer flags. Collages can also be done as three-dimensional objects, such as boxes, altars, or shadowbox constructions, for example, or as groups of pieces such as a deck of collage cards. Autumn Hathaway made a series of collage envelopes that are meant to be used for sending letters (see page 45). You may do many collage studies or sketches meant for your own personal reference and exploration, not to be viewed by others as finished pieces. These are all examples of format—another aspect of your work that informs its interpretation. It is another way in which you express meaning through collage.

FINDING MEANING IN THE JOURNEY

None of the above is to suggest that you have to justify every stroke of the brush or every decision about

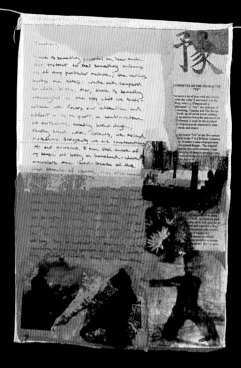
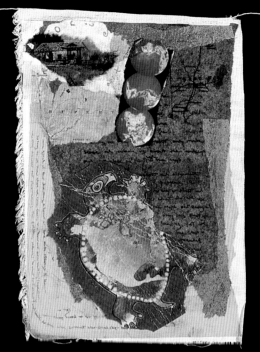

materials or technique by giving it a specific meaning. Far from it. This discussion is meant to inspire you to look at the rich territory of content that is already inherent in your collages if you are true to your intuitive sense of what "looks right" or "feels right" as you work. This should give you permission to use images that have personal meaning for you, even if you think they may be meaningless to someone else. It should also give you permission to exploit the vast wealth of meaning inherent in so many of our cultural symbols. You don't have to try to include both cultural and personal meanings in your collages. That just happens, whether you intend it or not. However, do give yourself room to experiment

Joshua Porter: Prayer flag collages on ecological identity
Joshua created a series of prayer flags to express a narrative about his ecological identity.

with the impact of different types of images, colors, materials, etc.

At some points along the journey your collage will reveal meaning, seemingly of its own accord, through unexpected juxtapositions of imagery. At other points you will nudge it along by making conscious choices about the direction of the journey. Allow this dialogue to unfold, and enjoy the ride!

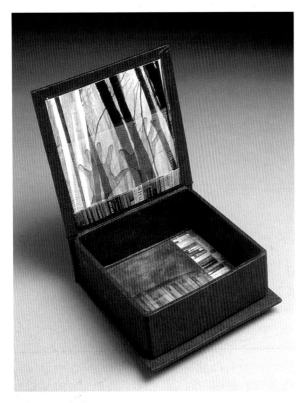

Jane Davies: My collage box
I made this box as a multi-part collage. I like the idea that the viewer has to handle it in order to experience the whole piece.

Autumn Hathaway: Spirit Dolls
I see Autumn's "Spirit Dolls" as a form of three-dimensional collage. Simply putting collage materials into a figure format gives them meaning and personality.

ABSTRACTION AND INTERPRETATION

Abstraction is focusing more on formal elements and less on a specific reference.

We sometimes refer to "abstract compositions" as opposed to representational imagery. What do we mean by "abstract"? In the visual arts, we usually use the term "abstract" to describe a piece that is not an image of something or that does not make specific reference to an object outside itself; instead it is an image that is to be interpreted on its own formal terms. However, even the most realistic photograph or painting is an abstraction of the object depicted in that it is a translation of a three-dimensional reality onto a two-dimensional surface. That said, there is a lot of gray area between an image that clearly depicts something and an abstract composition. Most pieces would fall into this gray area if we were to line them up on a continuum.

Let's look at this gray area. To abstract an image of something is to emphasize certain formal qualities and to eliminate certain details. For example, my collage "Merck Woods" is an abstraction of a photograph I took of the woods. I wanted to emphasize the uneven vertical lines of the trees and the atmospheric quality of the mist, and so I eliminated the details of horizontal branches, foliage, and background. Focusing more on formal elements—color, line, shape, value, etc.—and less on the specific reference (the object or scene depicted) is the essence of abstraction. Thus there are degrees of abstraction depending on the relative emphasis on formal and pictorial aspects of an image. Collage is a medium in which abstraction is particularly obvious, in that we often emphasize materials, patterns, textures, and surfaces. If you do choose to depict an image in collage, there is no expectation that it be realistic. That is an aspect of collage that makes it so accessible and immediate. (See my untitled collage and "Gallop Road," on page 119.)

Jane Davies: After the Explosion, 11˝ x 9˝
I included an image from the Halifax Explosion in this otherwise abstract composition, built up from layers of tissue paper, unryu, sumi paper, gesso, paint, and materials from my color stashes. I found these photographs documenting the explosion in Laura M. MacDonald's book *Curse of the Narrows*, a history of the event. Growing up in Halifax, I heard many stories of my peers' grandparents' survival of the catastrophe. I felt compelled to explore this material in a journal page, linking it to my own memories of Halifax in the 1970s. See my collage journey study on page 30.

Just as all image-making involves abstraction to one degree or another, all image-reading involves interpretation. Correlating an image to something outside itself, whether that is a specific object or simply a feeling or mood, is the essence of interpretation. Without its title, "Merck Woods" could as easily be interpreted as prison bars, not trees, or simply as a pattern of stripes. For some, it could merely evoke a mood and not a scene or object at all. Generally speaking, the more abstract an image is, the more it is open to interpretation. This is why text, context, and specific reference are so important to meanings in collage. You can specify meaning to whatever extent you choose.

als into an abstract composition. Like a Rorschach inkblot, the composition begins to suggest an image or evoke a mood. We may then choose to specify the image or mood by adding certain details or a title—something to direct its interpretation. For example, "After the Explosion" (page 117) and "High Tide" (page 84) are both essentially abstract compositions. Their titles direct their interpretation. This is taking the opposite approach from that of my "Merck Woods" collage. One can start with a specific reference, as I did for "Merck Woods," and abstract from there, or begin with an abstract composition, as I did with "After the Explosion" and impose specific (or not so specific)

Jane Davies: Merck Woods, 13˝ x 9 ½˝

A piece inspired by a misty day in the woods. I wanted to see if I could evoke the feeling of depth and mist by layering strips of dark paper and gesso.

Jane Davies: Photograph of Merck Forest

I took several photographs of the woods during a walk. This is the one that inspired the collage "Merck Woods."

Jane Davies: Untitled, 20˝ x 17˝
Jane Davies: Gallop Road, 20˝ x 17˝

In these two collages I used multiple printouts of "Merck Woods" as well as photographs and maps, all digitally resized and recolored, and printed on lightweight, translucent papers. The abstract and pictorial elements weave together to create visual ambiguity.

CHAPTER

7

JOURNALS AND JOURNEYS

Journal with no particular destination in mind.

What is a journey? How is it different from a trip? A journey can be physical travel in space, such as a hike or a plane ride. "Journey," as opposed to "travel," suggests the importance of the trip itself rather than the destination. When we speak of "journaling," we are similarly focusing on the process, not the outcome. When we journal we have no particular destination in mind. A diary is traditionally a daily (or periodic) record of What Happened, whereas a journal is much more open-ended. You can meander from one topic to another, making entries as the mood strikes you, go back over previous entries, or leave entries unfinished or questioning.

In chapter 2, we talked about how keeping a written journal is an integral part of the creative process. Now we'll consider visual journals, which can also incorporate writing and other text. First, let's consider the types of books you might choose to begin a collage journal.

BOOKS FOR COLLAGE JOURNALING

Choosing Blank Books
One way to start a collage journal is first to choose a blank book. It should not be elaborate or so expensive that you are afraid of ruining it. On the other hand, it should be substantial enough to withstand the gluing, painting, and writing that you will be doing in it. A few things to consider are:

- **Size.** Choose a size that feels comfortable—not so small that it feels confining, yet not so big that you are intimidated by The Blank Page.

Jane Davies: Double-page journal spread with added collage and painting
This is a double-page spread from my journal made from unbound collaged folios (see "Making a Book from Unbound Collaged Folios" on page 136) with added paint and collage.

- **Hard or soft cover.** Again, you should decide based on what feels comfortable or inviting to you. Either type of cover can be embellished with collage, writing, or painting. You can cut windows in either type or add pockets.
- **Binding.** A spiral-bound book lies flat more easily than a sewn or glued binding. However, it is hard to create continuous double-page spreads in a spiral-bound book; the spiral binding is always a visual as well as physical element.
- **Pages.** For collage journaling it is best to have reasonably sturdy paper so that it doesn't curl or buckle when you glue things to it. Most commercially made sketchbooks are adequate.

Altering an Existing Book
Another possibility for a collage journal is to use an existing book and alter it to your needs. To make an existing book into a sketchbook, find a sturdy discarded book at a flea market or used book store. A hardcover volume works best.

1. Tear out a few pages at regular intervals (every ten pages or so tear out two or three; the number of pages and the intervals depends on the individual book's pages) to make room in the spine for the added thickness of collage papers and paint you will be using. The photo shows pages I tore out to make room for collage in this altered book.

  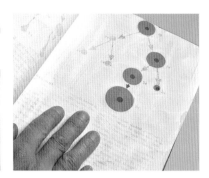

2. If the pages are of thin paper, laminate two or more of them together for each journal page. Or laminate some and leave others their original thickness. To laminate pages, first place a piece of scrap paper under one of the pages. Brush glue or matte medium evenly over the whole surface (the scrap paper will keep the glue from getting onto the other pages). Fold the facing page onto the glued page and burnish with a bone folder. Wipe away any excess glue with a damp paper towel. When laminating pages, make sure to apply glue all the way to the edge of the page, as shown in the photo on the left. In the center photo, I am burnishing the freshly laminated pages with a bone folder. You could also use a credit card, as described on page 27.

3. To prepare the pages for collage (this is optional), brush a coat of gesso, either straight or thinned with water or matte medium, onto each page. You can add more coats of gesso to completely obscure the text underneath, or leave some of it showing through. Another option is to gesso only parts of the pages, leaving the words, pictures, diagrams, or other elements that appeal to you as potential starting points for collage pages. Let each page spread dry thoroughly before going on to the next one. The book in the photo on the right had diagrams of chromosomes that appealed to me, so I left a few of them showing while applying gesso to the rest of the page.

You can prepare a whole book this way before using it as a collage journal, but you might find it easier or more approachable to tear, laminate, and gesso pages a few at a time as you go.

Handmade Journals

If you want to be a little more adventurous, try making a journal by hand. This allows you the freedom to choose your size, paper, and cover. The journal for which instructions are given starting on page 123 is easy to make and uses inexpensive materials. The instructions given are for a five-signature book, but you could make a series of one- or two-signature books if that seems more approachable.

There are as many ways to make a book as there are artists who make them. I have chosen this particular style of journal—a multi-signature, soft-cover book—because it is accessible to the novice book binder (it requires only one simple sewing stitch, used repeatedly), yet it produces a substantial, sturdy book to use for your collage journal. You can use plain papers for the cover or embellish it to your heart's content.

A *signature* is a group of folded sheets of paper nested into one another for the purpose of creating the pages of a book. Each of the folded sheets of paper is called a *folio*. A book can contain one or more signatures. The stack of signatures making up all the pages of a book is called the *text block*.

In this demonstration I use five signatures, but you could make more or fewer according to the number of pages you want in your book. Just remember to measure the stack of signatures to calculate the width of the spine. For the text block, I use 24″ x 18″ sulfite drawing paper, each sheet of which folds into a signature consisting of four folios that measure 9″ x 6″. Adjust the measurements if you want to use a different size of paper.

Project:
Making a Journal for Collage

You will need:

- Lokta or other heavy paper, in a solid color or patterned, for the inside cover
- Decorative or collaged paper for the outside cover
- Five sheets of medium-weight drawing paper for the signatures (each of which will become four folios), 24″ x 18″
- Waxed linen thread or embroidery floss stiffened with beeswax (dental floss, in a pinch)
- Sewing needle, awl or heavy-duty pushpin
- Glue and a glue brush

MAKE THE SIGNATURES

1. Using a paper cutter or folding and tearing with a bone folder, divide a sheet of drawing paper into quarters measuring 12″ x 9″.
2. Fold each quarter in half, and nest the four folios together to form a signature measuring 9″ x 6″.
3. Repeat with the remaining four sheets of paper. You should have five signatures each with four folios measuring 9″ x 6″.

Creating a signature
Several folios nested into one another form a signature.

MAKE THE COVER

1. The cover will measure the height of the text block plus a quarter inch for overhang (9¼˝), by twice the width of the text block (plus a quarter inch overhang) plus the width of the spine. For this journal that is six times two plus a quarter inch (12¼˝) plus the width of the spine, which is ⅝˝. This cover would measure 12⅞˝ x 9¼˝. You could round off this latter measurement to 13˝, and allow for a tiny bit more overhang on the front and back covers.

2. Cut your cover paper and lining papers to at least an inch more than the final measurements of the cover. Laminate them together by brushing glue (I use PVA with a little water added) on the back side of one sheet and laying the other sheet back side down on top of it. Cover with a sheet of wax paper and squeegee it with a bone folder or a credit card to get out any air bubbles and excess glue.

3. Let it dry, then cut the edges with a paper cutter or scissors to the correct size.

4. Find the middle of the spine by folding the cover in half and marking the center. Reinforce the spine by cutting an additional (possibly contrasting) strip of cover paper that is wide enough to wrap around the spine and overlap the front and back by an inch or so, and that is longer than the height of your cover. Glue it in place, and trim the top and bottom flush with the cover.

5. Make two folds ⅝˝ apart on either side of the center line. (You can eyeball this.) Reinforce the folds using a bone folder.

Two folds in the cover define the spine
Once you've finished laminating and cutting the cover, create the spine by making folds equidistant from the center. The width of the spine equals the height of the stack of signatures (the text block).

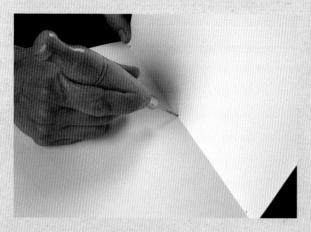

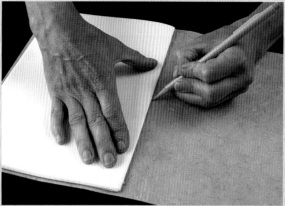

Punch holes in each signature with an awl

(1) Mark one signature along the spine to indicate where the sewing holes will be. Mark one hole in the center, and one on each end about half an inch from the top and bottom. (2) Using this as a guide, mark each signature on the inside fold, and punch holes using an awl or pushpin. Holding the signature open at a 90-degree angle over a scrap of foam core or a cutting mat, push the awl through at a 45-degree angle.

Marking the holes in the spine

Using the same guide centered along the spine of the cover, mark five holes, evenly spaced, at each location.

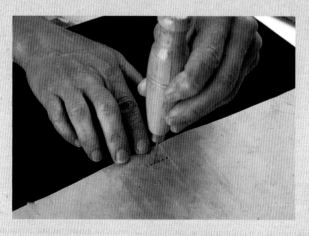

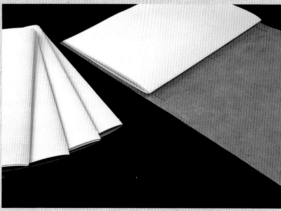

Punching the holes in the spine

Punch the holes using an awl or a heavy-duty pushpin.

Holes punched in the spine

The holes are all punched and you are ready to sew in the signatures.

SEWING THE SIGNATURES TO THE COVER

Beginning at the back of the book, place the first signature so that its sewing holes are lined up with those on the spine. Cut your thread three times the length of the spine. Thread your needle.

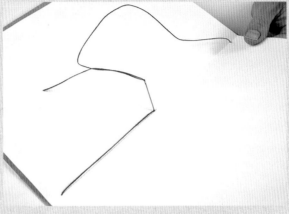

Sew in through the middle hole, out through the top hole
1. Starting from the outside of the book, sew in through the middle hole of the cover and signature, leaving a 6″ tail of thread. Sew out through the top hole, back in through the bottom hole.

Sew back through the bottom hole, and out through the middle
2. Then sew out again through the middle hole. Make sure the 2 threads coming out the back of the spine through the middle hole straddle the thread running along the spine.

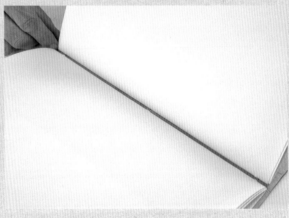

Come out through the middle hole; tighten everything up
3. Tighten everything up and tie a knot, leaving a tail of thread. Repeat the same process with the remaining four signatures.

The book interior between two signatures
4. The threads coming from the middle of the spine can be braided, tied, beaded, or cut short. Because of the soft spine, the book lies more or less flat when open.

The finished book
I chose black lokta paper to reinforce the spine of my book (see step 4 in "Make the Cover" on page 124) and after gluing it to the cover (before sewing in the signatures), I used my sewing machine to add a decorative zigzag stitch. I also stitched a stamped image of a dragonfly to the front cover.

THE COLLAGE SKETCH JOURNAL

The collage journal is like an artist's sketchbook. It is a playground for your ideas, a place to try techniques, experiment with materials and images, make sketches and notes for future projects, or simply express yourself visually as the mood strikes you. Like a written journal, a collage journal is a place where you can get your ideas out without trying to make them into finished compositions. The intimate nature of a journal, as opposed to a blank canvas, can allow you to loosen up and play freely. Nothing in your journal need ever be considered finished. The pages can remain works in progress to be revisited as many times as you like, and you don't need to fill them in order, front to back. Try starting somewhere in the middle, creating simple backgrounds with paper or paint.

JOURNALING PROJECTS

Maps

I titled my first entry in a recent collage journal "Personal Boundaries" (see page 77). I wanted to orient myself within the place I live in relation to my personal boundaries. I used road maps and U.S. Geological Survey maps of my town, Rupert, and nearby Tinmouth as a back-

Jane Davies: Journal page "Nenorod"
This journal page was a spontaneous response to a solitary walk in the woods to a cabin named "Nenorod." The November day was brilliant, chilly, and melancholy. In my journal, it doesn't matter to me if the feelings I express are communicated to another viewer. What matters is that I made a journal entry that speaks to me.

ground. I then drew a picture of my house on the edge of an imaginary body of water. Having grown up in Nova Scotia, with the ocean in sight everywhere, I have a visceral connection to large bodies of water. The page was a simple, direct response to feelings I was having about my privacy being invaded. It is a spare layout, inviting me to return to it with new ideas or perspective on personal boundaries.

On several other pages in this journal I start with maps of places that are significant to me. "Nenorod" is about a walk I took at Merck Forest, which has many miles of trails for hiking and skiing. Merck, which is only a few miles from my house, has become a very special place to me—usually a place for solitude and contemplative walks. The map fragments document actual walks in the woods there, but I also tried to capture some of my mood with watercolor, drawing, and writing. In "Chickadee," the map imagery was an excuse to try out Rowena Macleod's technique of layering watercolor crayon with magazine and other papers.

Jane Davies: Journal page "Chickadee"
"Chickadee" is the name of a trail at a nearby cross-country ski touring center. I had navigated it for the first time just before making the journal page.

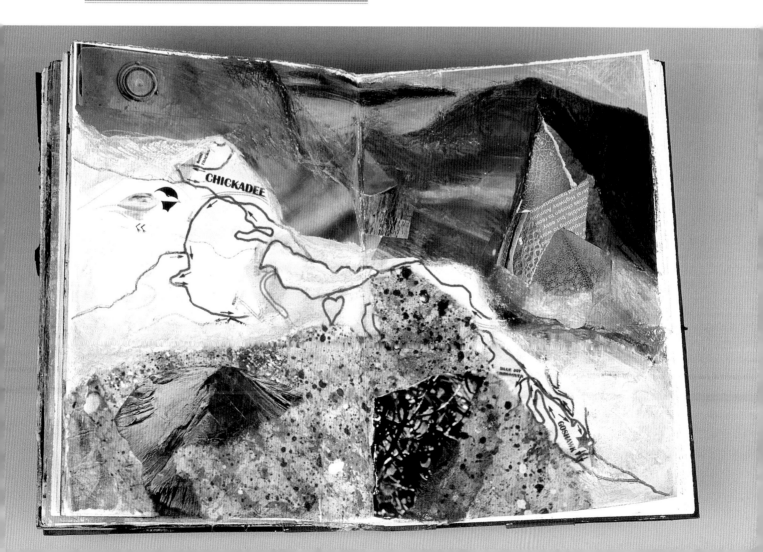

Gather some maps of places that are significant to you—street, road, contour, or any kind of map you like. Make a map collage in your journal, using maps of one or several places. Add some painting and drawing to establish a mood or a color scheme. Then use this as the basis for journaling about the place(s) or an event that happened in the place(s) described by the maps. You may come back to your map page at a later date and add bits of ephemera or journaling as other ideas occur to you. Again, you can consider your journal pages to be ongoing works in progress, always open to revision and addition.

A variation on this journaling exercise is to use maps of places that you haven't visited but that somehow intrigue you. I created the page entitled "Torngat Stories" as a response to a friend's description of the Torngat

Jane Davies: Journal page "Torngat Stories"
I scanned a map of the Torngat Mountains from my world atlas and printed it out onto lightweight mulberry paper. After gluing it down to the journal, I brushed water and diluted acrylic paint over selected areas, leaving the image blurred and unspecific. Then I added text taken from additional printouts of the map and wrote my thoughts on the facing page.

Mountains, a wild, barren mountain range along the coast of northern Labrador. I am fascinated by accounts of wild places. They evoke for me a sense of possibility, some hope that the planet is still fighting back.

Another variation you might try is to create a map of an imaginary place, either by piecing together actual maps or by drawing and painting. This could be a starting point for stories or reflections.

Using a Passage from Your Written Journal

I started my journal page called "Sitting" with a simple collage of pages from my written journal. I was writing about sitting with, and accepting, discomfort, when there is nothing to be gained by reacting to it otherwise. I wanted to think and write more about this in a visual way, yet I needed the page to reflect the austerity of the thoughts. Around the squares of journal pages, I cre-

ated the atmospheric texture by layering gesso, walnut ink, and acrylic wash until I had the desired effect. I did more journaling over the texture with a permanent marker. Then I shaded the top and side areas with black acrylic glaze to create a more mysterious feeling, and stamped the letters over that.

Choose a passage from your written journal that you would like to explore visually. Either make a simple composition in your collage journal using the original passage, as I did in "Sitting," or create a collage background and copy the passage onto it using any of the lettering techniques described in chapter 5. Choose colors and imagery that reflect the mood of your journal entry. If several different ideas about one passage come to mind, go ahead and start journal pages for each of them.

Jane Davies: Journal page "Sitting"
A passage from my writing inspired this journal page.

Journaling about an Activity That You Do or Would Like to Do

Autumn Hathaway created the double-page spread "Tumbling Blocks" (below) to reflect on her "inner quilter." In her journaling she reflects on her obsession with fabric and desire to make quilts, but also her fear of the skill and precision required to do so. In the end she decides that as a collage artist and journal keeper she can make paper "quilts."

Is there a hobby, sport, or profession that you think about but have never attempted? Have you fantasized about being a dancer, a mountain climber, a fashion model, or a rocket scientist? Your collage journal is the perfect place for you to play out this kind of fantasy or reflect on your thoughts about it. You might also create collage journal pages about activities that you do enjoy.

Autumn Hathaway: Journal double-page spread "Tumbling Blocks"
Autumn created these journal pages to reflect on her thoughts about quilting and her obsession with fabric.

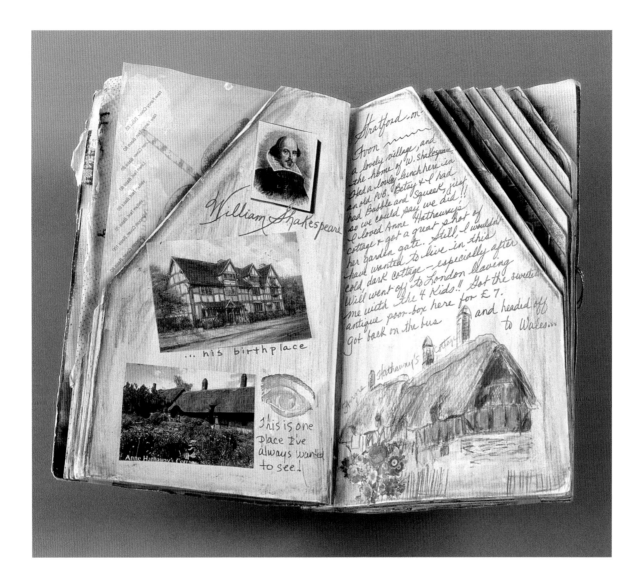

Stratford-on-Avon... a lovely village, and the home of W. Shakespeare. Had a lovely lunch here in an old Pub. Betsy & I had Bubble and Squeak, just so we could say we did!! I loved Anne Hathaway's cottage & got a great shot of her garden gate. Still, I wouldn't have wanted to live in this cold, dark cottage — especially after Will went off to London leaving me with the 4 Kids!! Got the sweetest antique poor-box here for £7. Got back on the bus and headed off to Wales...

William Shakespeare

...his birthplace

This is one Place I've always wanted to see!

Anne Hathaway's Cottage

Anne Hathaway's Cottage

MORE IDEAS FOR JOURNALING

A Day in the Life

Document your day with a series of photographs. This can either be a walk around your neighborhood, your city streets, or your backyard, or it can be just photographs of things you see throughout your day. Take your camera to work or on a morning walk. Get your film developed or print the images off your computer the same day. Collage them into your journal, taking up as many pages as you like. Add other collage elements; paint, draw, etc.; and write captions for each photograph. The captions may indicate the time and place of each photograph, your mood, your thoughts, or even found or invented text that gives your photographs a whole new context. You could also document a place, or event.

Dawne Polis: Ireland Journal
Dawne's book documents her recent trip to Ireland with her high-school students. It is very much like a traditional scrapbook or embellished photo album.

Word-Image Association

Try the word-image association project described in chapter 5 in your journal. Expand it to include images and text that you create as well as found images and text.

Jane Davies: Free-writing over collage journal page
This double-page spread in my collage journal, made from pre-collaged folios (instructions starting on page 136), seemed to suggest communication. It also had a lot of open space, making it the perfect page for a colorful free-write.

Collage Self-Portrait

Take a digital photo of yourself (a head shot works for this project) and print out multiple copies of it (resizing or recoloring if you wish). In your journal, make one or a series of self-portraits beginning with the photo and adding collage, painting, drawing, and writing. You can be as literal or as metaphorical, as silly or serious as you like. This is also a fun project to do in a group, where you have the option of passing around photos and making collage portraits of each other. You can do group portraits this way as well.

Free-Writing Over Collage

Make random collage and painted backgrounds in your journal and do the free-writing exercise from chapter 2 over them. Allow your writing to meander over the page, creating shapes and lines as well as words.

Autumn Hathaway: Journal page "Flowers"
Autumn made this journal page in the early spring when she was thinking about which flowers to plant.

TOPIC-SPECIFIC COLLAGE JOURNAL

Another approach to collage journaling is to create a book about a single topic. It could be partly documentary but might also include visual and textual musings on your topic. For example, a garden journal could document the development of your garden over a season or over the course of several years; it could also include your ideas about gardening in general, specific plants, events related to your garden, gardening metaphors and analogies—anything you associate with growing plants.

MAKING A BOOK FROM UNBOUND COLLAGED FOLIOS

This is a process of making unfinished spontaneous collages and then binding them into a book, creating unexpected double-page-spread compositions. Once the book is assembled, you continue to collage and paint (and write) on the resulting pages. This is an experimental exercise meant to challenge your ability to combine disparate elements, and to make meaning out of random combinations. It is a fun way to use up scraps or to experiment with new combinations of materials. It is also a great way to unleash your creative spontaneity.

Jane Davies: Journal double-page spread "Over the Deep End/ Coming Up for Air"
Another title from my idea list (see page 34).

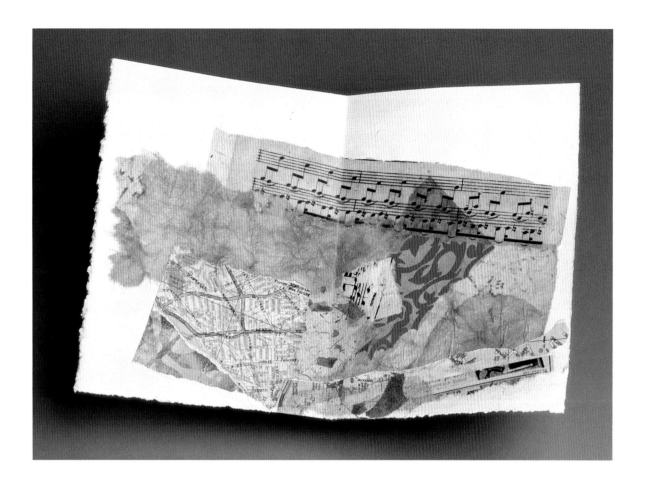

An unbound folio with random collage
This journal begins with a series of folios that are collaged
on both sides.

Make the Signatures

1. Choose a size that is comfortable for you to work
   with, and cut or tear your paper into sheets that are
   twice the width of your finished book. The number of
   sheets will depend on how many signatures you want
   in your book, and how heavy the paper is. You can
   nest more lightweight papers into a signature comfortably than you can heavier papers. For my folios
   I used a medium-weight printmaking paper, which is
   a bit more substantial than the sulfite drawing paper
   used in the blank book demonstration on page 123.
   I nested three folios into each of two signatures.

2. Collage, paint, and draw on both sides of each sheet
   of paper. You may choose to do this all in one sitting
   with one group of materials from your stash. This
   will give the book continuity or cohesiveness. On the
   other hand, you may choose to make the collages as
   different as possible, maximizing the surprising juxtapositions in the resulting double-page spreads.

3. Fold each piece of paper in half to make them into
   folios.

4. Make the folios into signatures by nesting them into
   one another in groups. Experiment with nesting them
   in different ways to create different double-page-
   spread layouts.

Sew the Signatures into the Cover

Following the instructions that start on page 125, mark and punch the holes in the signatures and book cover, and proceed to sew the signatures to the cover.

Now you are ready to use your journal as a collage playground. Each double-page spread offers something you can respond to. Collage, write, paint, sew, cut, tear. Not every spread will inspire you. You can always gesso over the collage material you've put down and start

Journal double-page spread
This is a double-page spread from the finished journal, ready for more collage, painting, writing, or any other creative application.

again. If you are intimidated by The Blank Page Syndrome, then this is a good way to start a collage journal. There aren't any blank pages!

Variations

1. Instead of using blank paper for the signatures, try using printed papers such as discarded maps, brochures, or patterned decorative papers. You might use a variety of papers within one journal. Simply bind these into a journal as is, or collage on them as described in the instructions above.

2. Instead of cutting sheets of paper for the folios first, begin by painting and/or collaging on several large sheets of paper, on both sides, and then cutting and folding them into folios.

Journal double-page spread
This double-page spread is continuous because it is on the inside of a signature.

Double-page spreads from paint/collage journal
Double-page spreads from variation 2 of the journal shown on
page 139.

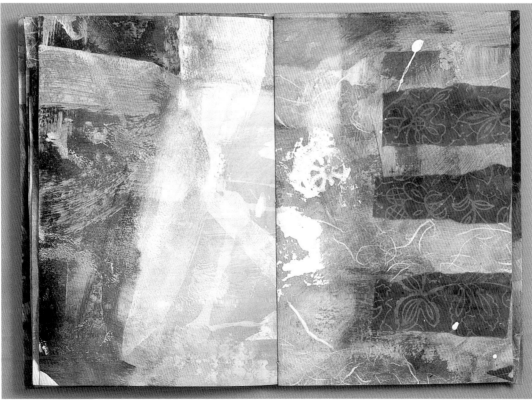

EPILOGUE

Collage is a practice. The more you do it, the more attuned you become to your own creative voice. No one can give you clear, step-by-step directions for making a collage that is truly your own. If you knew the destination in advance, the journey would be more like a commute, rather than the meandering, inquisitive route that makes collage so rich with possibility. The projects and practices I demonstrate in the preceding chapters are meant to engage your sense of journeying. Gathering and creating materials, making a collage every day, developing a visual vocabulary, spinning your wheels until something sparks your imagination, creating meaning through metaphor and personal iconography, and keeping a collage journal are just some of the practices that enhance your ability to articulate and express your ideas through collage.

Every collage artist I've interviewed has developed her own approach, style, and ways of working, but one thing they all have in common is their sense of the open-ended nature of the process—emphasis on *process*. This is what resonated with me and inspired me to write *Collage Journeys*. Each artist described her collage process as some variation of the following:

> You start *somewhere*, be it an idea, a group of materials, a technique, an image, anything at all. You play with it until it leads you to *somewhere else*. And so forth, until a theme or idea begins to develop, which suggests other ideas or materials lurking in the depths of your consciousness or the depths of your collage stash. You pull those out and start playing. So far you've been running on intuition, letting yourself respond on a gut level to what you are seeing. At this point you *stop and reflect on what you've done*. Somehow, the new combination suggests a larger idea you were working on three months ago, and you make a conscious decision to either go with that or take it back to its original direction. Once you make that decision, you return to the intuitive dialogue with your materials, until you reach another point of reflection and decision. . . .

And so it goes. Eventually your collage is finished, or it takes a rest for a few weeks or months until some resolution occurs to you. The process is a balance of letting things happen and making things happen, just like life. There is a time to go with the flow, and a time to reflect and make deliberate choices. The collage journey brings you to many forks in the road where you have to reflect on where you've been and decide where you are going. But along the way you can enjoy the scenery. I hope this book helps you tune into this balance, this ebb and flow, and enjoy the pleasures of your own collage journey.

ACKNOWLEDGMENTS

For me the most enjoyable part of writing a book is seeing it unfold as a collaboration. Indeed, it is quite a journey, from the initial concept to the final book design, requiring the input of many people, each putting their unique stamp on the project. I would like to thank Joy Aquilino, executive editor at Watson-Guptill, for her invaluable insights into the book's concept; the contributing artists for their generosity in allowing me to use their work and pick their brains about their own collage journeys: Cynthia Gregory, Autumn Hathaway, Alix Hegeler, Jane Maxwell, Sharon McCartney, Rowena Macleod, Kristen Mills, Dawne Polis, Erika Schmidt, and Sue Wright; my friends Melissa Patterson, Joshua Porter, and Mandy Smith for participating in "Collage Night"—our informal get-togethers during which we experimented with many of the techniques and projects in the book, and for contributing their work; John Polak and George Bouret for bringing the artwork to life with their skillful photography; my editor, Patricia Fogarty, for her meticulous hard work; and Chin-Yee Lai and Wendy Lai for their creative and insightful book design. I would also like to thank my parents, Beverly and Jim Davies, for their help with manuscript revisions; and my love, John LaVecchia, for his moral support and constant encouragement.

Collage envelopes by Autumn Hathaway

INDEX